ELIZABETH OF THE TRINITY

SISTER GIOVANNA DELLA CROCE, O.C.D.

Translated by Julie Enzler

Elizabeth
OF THE
Trinity

SOPHIA INSTITUTE PRESS

Manchester, New Hampshire

Elizabeth of the Trinity is a translation of *Elisabetta della Trinità: una vita di lode* (Milano: Figlie di San Paolo, 1993).

Printed in the United States of America. All rights reserved.

Cover design by Perceptions Design Studio.

Cover photograph courtesy of the Carmel in Dijon-Flavignerot.

Sophia Institute Press
Box 5284, Manchester, NH 03108
1-800-888-9344

www.SophiaInstitute.com

Sophia Institute Press® is a registered trademark of Sophia Institute.

Library of Congress Cataloging-in-Publication Data

Names: Giovanna della Croce, OCD, author.
Title: Elizabeth of the Trinity / Sister Giovanna della Croce, O.C.D. ; translated by Julie Enzler.
Other titles: Elisabetta della Trinità. English
Description: Manchester, New Hampshire : Sophia Institute Press, 2016. | Includes bibliographical references.
Identifiers: LCCN 2016029812 | ISBN 9781622823772 (pbk. : alk. paper)
Subjects: LCSH: Elizabeth of the Trinity, Sister, 1880-1906 | Christian saints—France—Biography. | Carmelite Nuns—France—Biography. | Mystics—France—Biography.
Classification: LCC BX4705.E44 G5613 2016 | DDC 271/.97102 [B]—dc23 LC record available at https://lccn.loc.gov/2016029812

First printing

CONTENTS

FOREWORD

We need the life of praise. In the twentieth century, a renewal of spiritual teaching helped the Church proclaim that only a gaze that searches for God discovers the truth about our humanity and the greatness of the particular calling each of us has received. Conversely, without a wholehearted return to prayer to God, all that is tender and good in life is at risk. The spiritual wisdom of St. Elizabeth of the Trinity contributed to this important teaching, and her canonization comes at a time when her witness and message are most needed.

We are all survivors of a society that is quickly losing sight of what is most essential and beautiful about life. We are suddenly coming to realize that the very heart of our culture is now hardened. Grasping for some real encounter, we amuse ourselves to death with cold and lifeless technology only to discover how disconnected we have become. We are schooled in all forms of tolerance even as we lose the capacity for friendship and sincerity with one another. Because we have averted our gaze from the Source of Life, our relationships, even in the intimacy of marriage and family, cannot find the warmth and light that they need to thrive.

While our noisy culture and our fragmented personal lives are spiraling out of control, a Carmelite mystic reminds us about God's power to establish us in a profound and peaceful stillness. While all kinds of social, political, and psychological strife tear at us, she has a mission to remind us that the Lamb has already won the victory. While we feel alienated and disconnected, she proclaims that there is "a Being who is Love" who remains with us and that the Trinity is none other than our true home, the bosom where we are awaited with love. From the vantage point that she gained through God's work in her, even in this time of social cacophony, she invites us to rediscover the simple joy of deep prayer, adoration, and praise.

In my last conversation with Father Jordan Aumann, O.P., at the Angelicum, he expressed concern that spiritual theologians had not yet really understood or explored the doctrine of Elizabeth of the Trinity. He lamented the fact that most approaches to the Mystic of Dijon had imposed theological frameworks extrinsic to her works without really understanding her distinctly Carmelite worldview. He insisted that better explorations of her doctrine would come from those who would enter into her thought with greater humility and explore the questions that her Carmelite spirituality evokes. He was suggesting a more empathetic and interiorized approach to her wisdom.

This is what Sister Giovanna della Croce, O.C.D., achieves in this present, brief, and insightful introduction to the teachings of Elizabeth of the Trinity. Until now, however, this work could be accessed only by an Italian and Carmelite readership. On the eve of her canonization, Julie Enzler's adept translation of this work provides access for the English-speaking world to this important starting point for understanding the spiritual mission of Elizabeth of the Trinity.

This work and the translation provided in these pages are themselves the products of personal prayer and the spiritual mission of St. Elizabeth of the Trinity at work in the Church in our time. Several years ago, I asked Mrs. Enzler's assistance in translating a portion of this text for private use in my research. As a mother and wife, Mrs. Enzler also found encouragement in the writings of St. Elizabeth and in Sister Giovanna's presentation of her teachings. In no time, she produced a preliminary translation of this spiritual goldmine. Now revised and carefully edited, this work promises to be a blessing for everyone seeking authentic contemplative prayer.

There are several reasons for this. First, Sr. Giovanna's text conveys an empathetic exploration of the mystical wisdom that lives at the heart of the Carmelite vocation. She shares deeply in the same alignment of doctrine, mental prayer, and life that Carmel proposes to the Church and that lives in the spiritual wisdom of Blessed Elizabeth. Sister Giovanna's work and Mrs. Enzler's translation of it share in Blessed Elizabeth's feminine genius, a genius that can come only from the heart of the Church, the vantage point of being a living icon of the Church's bridal reality.

Sister Giovanna della Croce, O.C.D., is a Carmelite nun in a contemplative Carmelite convent in Milan. She is a brilliant intellectual. Her pursuit of the truth led her, as it did other intellectuals, to the contemplative life and to the mystery of the Carmelite vocation. Like many contemplatives, however, she discovered the magnetism of the writings of Elizabeth of the Trinity, and she presents her powerful insights in this volume.

If scholars such as Father Conrad De Meester, O.C.D., describe Elizabeth's writings as "a mosaic in the apse," Sister Giovanna della Croce helps us appreciate the sacred truths portrayed in this mosaic of biblical, patristic, medieval, and modern piety. Like an apse over a sanctuary, the writings of the Carmelite of Dijon surround a sacred space of encounter in which Christ comes anew for the Church. Within her message, one discovers a holy meeting place in which the soul suddenly finds itself enveloped by the life of the Trinity. The kind of contemplation to which she directs us rises above mere private acts of piety or the exercise of devout emotions and religious fantasy. Authentic contemplative prayer flows from and leads to the liturgy: grounded by baptism in this drama of praise unfolding in the heavens above, prayer extends the ways we participate in this mystery now, here below.

In this exploration, Sister Giovanna gives us insight into "Laudem Gloriae," the name that St. Elizabeth believed was hers in heaven. Having mastered the Carmelite tradition, especially in its twentieth-century expression, Sister Giovanna helps us appreciate our new saint's mission to lead souls out of themselves and into heavenly and eternal realities. We come to see that heaven is not simply a future hope, but a present reality, beginning and progressing already in time.

Sister Giovanna is particularly aware of how this spiritual wisdom is not limited to the convent, but something that expands to the whole life of the Church. Since St. Elizabeth first discovered this prayer as a teenager and laywoman, she does not view such contemplation as the privilege of a religious elite. Instead, she would that this kind of prayer be sought by all, whether married or single, consecrated or discerning, priest or lay, young or old.

Out of a love that is stronger than death, we have every reason to believe that St. Elizabeth of the Trinity is accompanying us spiritually today in the midst of the difficult circumstances and trials that we face. She believed, like St. Thérèse of Lisieux, that she would not spend her heaven indifferent to the plight of her friends. She came to realize how much we need personal intimacy and real friendship with the Lord, no matter what our vocation is. If, in the face of our times, the Church has asked us to become missionary disciples who lead others into an authentic encounter with the Lord, these pages will help us to appreciate why St. Elizabeth of the Trinity is ready to help us answer this call.

—Dr. Anthony Lilles
Co-founder, the Avila Institute
Academic Dean of Saint John's Seminary
Camarillo, California

ELIZABETH OF THE TRINITY

INTRODUCTION

The beginning of Elizabeth's life, ten years after the fall of the Napoleonic Empire, coincided with a difficult period for the Church in France.

It was 1880. As was the case in the rest of Europe, the consequences of the anticlerical prejudice of a government that would soon proceed to violent manifestations against religion could be felt. Many remembered these sad times of the Revolution of 1789.

If, in the early years of the Third Republic, most of the bourgeoisie still held positions of influence in the courts of law and in the military, as did Elizabeth's father, Catholics could not ignore the strengthening of masonic lodges as centers of promotion of a new secular ideal, foreign to the Christian faith. Priests and actively committed laypeople were too weak to oppose the new ideas that were directed toward liberating the human spirit from "religious darkness." The anticlerical politics of the government gained the upper hand with a strong propaganda slogan: it was time to grasp society by the "clerical yoke." Especially the working class was involved, thus contributing to widespread systematic secularization.

To this were added the Modernist crisis within the Church in France and tensions created by the American New Deal.[1]

---

[1] Although Franklin D. Roosevelt would announce the New Deal almost thirty years after St. Elizabeth of the Trinity's death, Sister Giovanna is accurately suggesting that the anticlerical

To understand the situation it is enough to read Charles Péguy, rightly considered "a chronicler of French disbelief at the end of the 19th century."[2] Increasingly intense conflicts last until the first world war, to the point that "France [became] mission territory,"[3] becoming a country in which a new conformism replaced the old and everything that concerned religion was left behind.

This was the France of Elizabeth Catez.

In 1875, with the definition of the composition of the republic, good Catholics nurtured hopes that the new government would

---

tendencies in France coincided with anti-Catholic attitudes in America at the time. Similar to the leaders of France's Third Republic, many of those with political power in America during and after Reconstruction and those in its growing university system presumed that national progress would be fostered the more government could limit the influence of Catholic Institutions. In particular, President Grant associated the Catholic Faith with "superstition." He and other leaders, including future presidents Hayes and Garfield, stated explicitly that the growing number of Catholic immigrants and the Catholic school system posed threats to the future progress of the country. Long after Grant left office, his prejudice fed legislative efforts to tax and limit the Church, including the Blaine Amendment, which paralleled political efforts in France throughout St. Elizabeth's lifetime. For a general discussion on American political opinion toward the Church in the late nineteenth century, see John T. McGreevy, *Catholicism and American Freedom: A History* (New York: Norton, 2003), pp. 91–105.—Trans.

[2] P. Duployé, *La religion de Péguy* (Paris, 1965), pp. 13–17.

[3] This expression was heard in France beginning in 1893. Fr. Carlo Calippe used it in his *Diary*, and Poulat so titled one of his chapters in a presentation (from the Italian translation *Diario di un prete di dopodomani* [Rome, 1971], p. 43).

restore a balance to France's social and economic evolution. But already in 1880, with the so-called republican defense[4] the new political direction was clearly revealed through the handing down of a series of decrees and abhorrent laws that were hostile to the Church. In fact, fearing the influence of the Catholic Church present throughout France in schools and charitable works, the government decreed the closing of 261 men's monasteries, reserving a particular hostility for the Jesuits.

In 1882 a new law removed the obligation of religious instruction in school, and shortly thereafter the religious neutrality of schools was defined in a very restrictive way with the exclusion of men and women religious from teaching.

The secularization of schools kept pace with the profaning of religious symbols in hospitals and public buildings. From Rome, Pope Leo XIII tried in vain to save the situation with an invitation to form a conservative party for Catholics and all "honest men," based on religious liberty to pass new laws and slowly modify the anticlerical decrees. These very same Catholics, however, had insufficient preparation to accept the pope's proposal, even though efforts to avoid the break between the Church and the state continued until 1890. Unfortunately, that same papal politic of *ralliement* causes the separation between Rome and France in 1905.

The anticipated fall of the Church did not happen.

French Catholicism had been experiencing a spiritual renaissance for the past ten years, thanks to a group of priests who,

[4] "Supporters of the Republican Defense viewed most Catholic orders ... as subversive forces injurious to healthy political progress." Robert Lynn Fuller, *The Origins of the French Nationalist Movement, 1886–1914* (Jefferson, NC: McFarland, 2012), p. 180.—Trans.

stimulated by Leo XIII's directives, became followers of George Pierre Fonsegrive-Lespinasse (1852–1917)[5] who was working to "acclimate French Catholics to modernity" in conformity with scientific progress. In the 1890s "the wind of Pentecost" began to blow more strongly through the action of Charles Maurras (1868–1952)[6] and his foundation Action Française (1899), on which many French Catholics, not only conservatives, placed their hopes.

Even with these initiatives, French Catholics remained upset by the spread of the biblical-theological writings of Alfred Loisy (1857–1940).[7] In his books, Loisy had the audacity to challenge the Church's traditional positions, distressing the consciences of some believers with the idea that Jesus would not have come to organize a new religious society destined to prolong His work, begun with the preaching of the Kingdom of God, but only to announce the next reestablishing of the reign of God. The Church, on the other hand, presupposing the fulfillment of the messianic advent, gave it form and structure, losing sight of the fact that the essence of Christianity was not to be found in the present but in the yet-to-come.

Weak assertions these, and dangerous — with the goal of destroying the Catholic Church? Rome could not remain silent and, in the end, condemned Loisy's writings.

---

[5] Author of two works, *Lettres d'un curé de champagne* (1894) and *Journal d'un évêque* (1896), and director of the magazine *Cahiers de la quinzaine*.

[6] See A. Cormier, *La vie intérieure de Charles Maurras* (Paris, 1956).

[7] Albert Houtin, Felix Sartiaux, and Émile Poulat, *Alfred Loisy: sa vie, son oeuvre* (Paris: Éditions du Centre national de la recherche scientifique, 1960).

After this, at the turn of the century, despite Leo XIII's and Pius X's repeated interventions, the Modernist crisis, today considered to have been almost necessary, exploded. Preachers put the faithful on guard about accepting theories that apparently reconciled the modern world with traditional Catholicism, but they could not prevent a certain number of Catholics from desiring a serious updating of some ecclesial institutions, of pastoral approaches, and of the style of Christian life, more in conformity with the reality of a French society "young and full of new life."

The France of the 1800s gloried in new inventions and discoveries in every field.

First of all, advances made in the field of technology helped French religious spread the Faith overseas. Missionaries, today severely criticized because they are judged as uncultural and wrong, worked zealously side by side with colonists. For the general population, the missionary colonists served to enlarge their view, making it broader, more universal, tearing them from the confines of a middle-class mentality. The effect on society was notable, as it was on the economic level with the importation of riches and prime materials.

In the field of art, including sacred art, expressions of new styles emerge. It is the age of the Gothic renaissance, better than the neo-Gothic, which included imitations that were not always faithful. It was considered a "progressive" style, and now new churches were no longer being built by artistically gifted monks, but by technically trained laity. They even wanted to call the neo-Gothic style the "lay style."[8] These popular elements were

---

[8] See Eugène di Viollet-le-Duc, ed., *Dictionnaire raisonné de l'architecture française* (Paris, 1854–1968), 1:114, and in following of common usage.

also manifested in music and painting. The ideals of the Nazorean style were reflected in paintings of a sentimental genre. Nostalgia to reach increasingly surreal destinations gave life to a style of musical composition that strongly played on the emotions.

The extreme variety of initiatives that characterized French Catholicism and the awakening of progressive ideas that marked the end of the 1800s served as the background of the earthly adventures of our Carmelite of Dijon, Elizabeth Catez.

Before entering the Carmelite cloister, Elizabeth lived like most of her peers. She participated in concerts, small dance parties, hikes in the mountains, and tennis. She did not want for marriage proposals either.

As an excellent pianist, she received success and applause, won competitions, and cherished the little pleasures of a girl full of life. She absorbed the contrasts of her century: artistic ideals, dreams, determination to reach goals, and the overcoming of bourgeois and conservative influences. But deep within her vibrated a longing for silence and solitude, a place where she could seek and find absolutes.

Elizabeth was in tune with the mentality of her century. Even if she had an insufficient cultural and intellectual formation to be able to follow well the goings-on of French politics and Church problems, she was not deprived of a glorious openness toward those modern realities that unleash the greatest forces of contemporary Catholicism.

She was not an atypical figure; nor was she a contemplative monastic who could be inserted into just any period of history; nor could she be spoken of simply as "the saint of silence and interior recollection." This young woman lived an immense love for the destiny of France. In a poem composed at age seventeen, in September 1897, she expresses her pain at the distancing of her fellow countrymen from the Church. To Joan of Arc, the *humble petite bergère*, in that period a focus of French Catholic interest and the protagonist of a book by Charles Péguy, Elizabeth begged intercession from heaven to bring faith to their land.

> France, dear country, most beloved, most beautiful.
> What torment to watch you rebel against your Lord!
> May the humble little shepherdess,
> That famous warrior, the glorious saint, restore you.
>
> From her eternal homeland, the heroic Maiden
> Give you back faith, obtain your victory,
> Among the most beautiful, forgiving your errors,
> Conquering your freedom.
> O my homeland, beloved France,
> For you am I consecrated to the Lord![9]

---

[9] This poem was not footnoted by the author, nor has any number reference been given, and, to the best of this translator's knowledge, only twenty of Elizabeth's poems have been published in English. These poems are collected in *Barb of Fire: Twenty Poems of Blessed Elizabeth of the Trinity with selected passages from Blessed Columba Marmion, OSB*, trans. Alan Bancroft (Herefordshire: Gracewing, 2001). — Trans.

CHAPTER ONE

A SIMPLE LIFE: BETWEEN MUSIC AND SILENCE

An Ordinary Young Woman

Elizabeth Catez was born on July 18, 1880, in the military camp at d'Avor, near Bourges, in the heart of France. The small church where she was baptized on July 22, the feast of St. Mary Magdalene, still stands. She would always remember the anniversary of her baptism, the day she became "adopted daughter sealed with the sign of the Holy Trinity." In a letter to Reverend Chevignard she wrote, "Tomorrow ... is the anniversary of my baptism, and since you are a minister of Love, I ask you ... to want to *consecrate me* truly to Jesus tomorrow at holy Mass. Baptize me in the blood of the Lamb so that virgin of all that is not He, I [will] live with an ever-increasing passion only for love until [I reach] that happy *unity* to which God has predestined us in His eternal and unchanging will."[10]

---

[10] To Reverend Chevignard, L234, July 21, 1905, in *Gli Scritti*, pp. 358–359. For citations and "selected works" in part V, compare Elisabetta della Trinity, *Gli Scritti*, care of the Postulation OCD (Rome, 1967). The translation underwent numerous

When she was born, her father was forty-eight years old. Francis Joseph Catez came from the north of France, from Jumelle. He was an officer in the army overseeing the Sixteenth Squadron of equipment services. Elizabeth only just remembered him because he died on October 2, 1887, after a long, painful illness, which he bore with peace and a smile. She remembered him with veneration. Before her entrance into Carmel she prayed before his portrait to ask for his blessing.[11] On the tenth anniversary of his death she composed a poem with fleeting references to her childhood.[12]

Elizabeth's mother, on the other hand, was from the south of France. Marie Rolland, of Lunéville, was married on September 3, 1879. She was thirty-three years old, fifteen years her husband's junior. She would be mother to two girls, Elizabeth, the firstborn, and Guite (Marguerite). Possessive by nature, Madame Catez loved her daughters passionately, especially Elizabeth, whose plan to be a Carmelite she opposed with all her strength.

Elizabeth's early childhood—ten months at the garrison of Avor and eighteen at Auxonne, finally settling in Dijon—was a happy one.

The family lived in an elegant villa on Lamartine Avenue, where Guite was born in 1883. They wanted for nothing, until the day Elizabeth's maternal grandfather died and shortly

---

modifications. The numbering of the letters, retreats, and poems and the respective dates always correspond to those of the critical work: Elisabeth de la Trinité, *J'ai trouvé Dieu. Oeuvres complètes*, vols. Ia, Ib, II (Paris: Éditions du Cerf, 1980).

[11] Germaine of Jesus, *Suor Elisabetta della Trinità religiosa carmelitana 1880–1906*, 4th ed. Ricordi (Florence, 1942), p. 79. Later cited in Ricordi.

[12] Poem 37, October 2, 1897, in *Gli Scritti*, pp. 686–687.

thereafter her beloved father. The widow and her two young daughters moved to a more modest apartment on Prieur-de-la-Côte-d'Or. Madame Catez dedicated herself to her daughters' education—no easy task thanks to Elizabeth's strong character and iron will, which she had inherited from her father. She always tried to get what she wanted, and she would not bow to anyone else's will. Unbearable, even irascible, but at the same time sensitive and full of tenderness: this is how her sister remembered Elizabeth as a child. Her mother, thanks to her giftedness as a teacher, was able to guide her along the right path and to "persuade her for love's sake" to allow herself to be guided by grace. Elizabeth's first confession precipitated her first conversion, as she later affirmed. At her First Communion a new life began in her, thanks in part to the good preparation by her parish priest, who, somewhat frightened by Elizabeth's temperament, had declared that she would become "either a saint or a demon."

April 19, 1891, the day of her First Communion, was of fundamental importance in Elizabeth's life. After receiving Jesus in the Church of St. Michael in Dijon, Elizabeth seemed to hear Jesus' voice calling her to be wholly His. How? At only eleven years old, she understood the need to begin to guard against her angry explosions and to put into practice the resolution she made to her mother in a note on New Year's Day, 1889. "Dear Mommy, wishing you a happy new year, I want to promise that I will be very good and obedient, that I won't make you angry and I won't cry anymore, and I will be a good girl and make you happy in everything. Maybe you don't believe me, but I will do everything I can to keep my promises."[13] After receiving Jesus in her First Communion she felt gripped by Him and strengthened

---

[13] To her mother, L4, January 1, 1889, in *Gli Scritti*, p. 63.

in her resolve to overcome her fiery temper. This battle would accompany her for ten years, and perhaps until her death. It was precisely her inborn tenacity to finish whatever she began that helped her in this.

Elizabeth grew up like most girls from good, middle-class families. She spent her summers between visiting the Alps, the seaside, Switzerland, and Lourdes and Paris. "I love these mountains that I see," she wrote from Tarbes, and she thought about taking a long trip "through the Pyrenees, Luchon, Cauterets, et cetera." She added, "I think I have to do it!"[14] In her excursions in the Jura Mountains she immersed herself in listening to nature's voices, to melodies traced on blank pages, carried along by flashes of delicate observations.[15]

The letters recounting her trip to the seaside are full of remarks about the enchanting skies and the running waters that invite her to contemplate the marvels of creation. "We spent the morning at the beach admiring the sea, so enticing to me!"[16] A year before her entrance at Carmel she wrote from Biarritz that she experienced a quasi-ecstasy from the orchestra of the ocean waters. "What beauty!... I am unable to describe this grand spectacle. The endless horizon fascinates my spirit! Mother and Guite were unable to tear me from my contemplation, perhaps

[14] To Alice Chervau, L14, July 21, 1898, in *Gli Scritti*, p. 63.

[15] Elizabeth's memories of her *Excursions in the Jura Mountains* of August–September 1895 can be found in *Gli Scritti*, pp. 509–515: the Rocks of Sirod, Lake Chalain, the falls at Planches, Mount Rivel, Balerne, Berta. These are certainly youthful gushings, but in their simplicity these declarations reflect a great love of nature and an uncommon ability to describe the places she had seen and deeply appreciated.

[16] To Mlle. Fory, her tutor, L12, ca. August 10, 1896, in *Gli Scritti*, p. 69.

they found my reaction a bit exaggerated."[17] From her letter to Madamoiselle Forey it seems she would have liked to dive into the sea, swim against the surf, or let the waves of a calm sea roll over her. "I envied the delight of the swimmers."[18] Dreams, contemplations, gentle memories that escape in brief lyrical verses:

> When on the welcoming shores
> Dashing at my feet
> The blue waves come
> It is nice to dream and pray![19]

But she does not run from reality; she does not want to lose herself in an idealized world of desires. At summer's end she does not close herself to the call of the present.

> Goodbye, dear vacation!
> Rich in emotions.
> Goodbye! School returns,
> Sweet and precious toil![20]

For Elizabeth school meant, first of all, pianoforte.

Her mother, desirous for her daughter to become an artist, rather than obliging her to serious study of literature and the sciences, preferred to limit her academic instruction to private lessons. Time to practice the piano came before everything else.

Elizabeth succeeded brilliantly at the Dijon Conservatory. She possessed all the necessary qualities to execute even difficult pieces perfectly. She was gifted with a particular musical

---

[17] To Mlle. Maria Luisa Maurel, Aude L30, August 12, 1900, in *Gli Scritti*, p. 101.

[18] To Mlle. Forey, L12.

[19] Poem 14, September 23, 1894, in *Gli Scritti*, p. 675.

[20] Poem 15, September 24, 1894, in *Gli Scritti*, p. 675.

sensitivity, a subtlety of interpretation, and an expressive facility in emphasizing a musical phrase, measure, rhythm, or chord. But she was no genius. Those who knew her said that her sister Guite was more gifted than she was. In any case, it is necessary to note that Elizabeth took her piano studies seriously and was extremely self-disciplined. Her constant progress, her passion for music, and her frequent mastery earned her admiration and esteem, forming her character and behavior, as she aimed for success. Her tendency to dress stylishly was also noted. "Elizabeth was very elegant, admirably dressed and her hair nicely done," said Françoise de Sourdon, finding herself next to Elizabeth at an evening reception for General Massiet. "She truly knew how to dress! She always wanted to have what was in fashion, and every once in a while she asked her mother to buy her this or that item."[21]

Sometimes the Catez sisters would play a duet at a reception. People would whisper, "Absolutely enchanting, these two sisters!" And they would shower the girls with praise. The pieces they performed were from the composers of the era: Chopin, Liszt,[22] Schumann.

The most difficult pieces were performed at concerts organized by the Dijon Conservatory. In 1893 Elizabeth won first

---

[21] Cf. M. D. Poinsenet, *Questa presenza di Dio in te* (Milano, 1971), p. 82.

[22] Guite was also very talented. In fact, at the July 25, 1896, concert she won (*prix d'excellence*) after playing Liszt's *Spanish Rhapsody* "avec une sûreté, une maestrie, une entente des intentions du compositeur tout à fait étonnantes" (with surety, mastery, and an amazing intuition of the composer's intentions). The August 4 newspaper brings to light the fact that she is only thirteen. (*Elisabeth de la Trinité, J'ai trouvé Dieu, Oeuvres complètes*, vol. 2 [Paris, 1979], p. 150, no. 4.) Elizabeth mentions this in a letter to Alice Chervau, August 1896 (*Gli Scritti*, p. 68).

place with unanimous applause after playing *Capriccio brillante* by Mendelssohn. The August 8 edition of *Le Progrés de la Côte-d'Or* did not fail to praise the young pianist, in whom great hope could rightly be placed.[23]

Elizabeth also acquired a discrete artistic formation. She knew sacred music such as Gounod's[24] "O Salutaris Hostia" and Charles-Camille Saint-Saens' *Trio*.[25] She also composed some religious songs with accompaniment.[26] She did not dislike the popular music typical of her time, played for dancing, and she enjoyed dancing to the lively and spontaneous sequences of the waltz and folk dances.

And yet she was ready to sacrifice everything for a greater calling. The song of a mysterious lyre had long whispered the invitation to Carmel. "I never thought of anything beside Carmel. And I would willingly sacrifice my piano."[27] For her, "the attraction of Carmel is a force that nothing can block, not even

---

[23] Cf. *J'ai trouvé Dieu*, vol. Ib (Paris, 1980), p. 14. After receiving first place, Elizabeth should have gone to Paris for further studies, but she preferred to continue her private lessons and studies in music theory at the Dijon Conservatory for two years. In her free time she tried to complete her academic formation, studying English and taking sewing lessons.

[24] In Carmel she asked her sister to copy the music and send it to her for an upcoming feast. To Guite, L119, before June 15, 1902, in *J'ai trouvé Dieu*, vol. Ib, p. 87.

[25] To Guite, L118, before August 15, 1902, in *J'ai trouvé Dieu*, vol. Ib, p. 86.

[26] After her signature she notes, "I composed a vocal piece that will be sung on the feast of the Assumption." To Alice Chervau, L9, ca. August 10, 1896, in *Gli Scritti*, p. 69.

[27] Postulation of her Cause, *Elisabetta parla ancora* (Rome, 1980), no. 40.

the love she feels for her mother."[28] Her mother, on the other hand, nurtured a dream for her daughter to marry and therefore violently opposed the idea of Elizabeth's entering a monastery, which would make it difficult for her to immerse herself in the world of music.

THE VOCATION TO CARMEL

In the afternoon of the day of her First Communion, April 19, 1891, not far from her home on rue Carnot, Elizabeth and her mother met the sisters of Carmel for the first time.

From behind the grille Mother Mary of Jesus smiled and thought of the sisters' new foundation at Paray-le-Monial. During their conversation, she said to Elizabeth, "What a nice name! Elizabeth, house of God." A little while later, as if to mark their encounter, Mother gave her a holy card on which she had written a few lines inviting the young girl to reflect on the mystery of her name.

Elizabeth's name already pointed to her vocation to Carmel. She would later add only "of the Trinity," so as to live, day after day, the reality of the divine indwelling.

Her choice to be a Carmelite began to take shape in her heart after a Eucharistic experience she had when she was fourteen. She seemed to hear in her heart the echo of a voice whispering, "Carmel." She did not hesitate in answering, and a vow of virginity blossomed from her spirit as a commitment to belong to God alone. She desired to suffer with Jesus, to unite herself

---

[28] Ibid., no. 39.

to the Bridegroom through suffering. It was a desire and a commitment that settled her vocation. She wrote:

> I want to possess You, my Jesus
> I wait only to be Your bride.
> With You I want to suffer,
> To find You and then die.[29]

Any attempt to speak with her mother failed. She thought that Elizabeth's musical talent would bring worldly success, and now that France was full of new inventions, religious life seemed doomed to die out. Forced to renounce her desire, Elizabeth intensified her interior life by committing to live constantly in the Lord's presence interiorly. Unattached to her life in the world, she tried to discover the presence of Christ everywhere. "It was not I who played," she said to someone who complimented her after an excellent execution of a piece. "He played for me."[30]

Her life of union with Christ allowed her to conquer true interior freedom. Her sensitivity to the positive influence of music and poetry opened her to divine grace and aided her in acquiring virtue. So that I "might delight my Beloved," resembling, "a walled garden where Jesus loves to stay," and always doing His will.[31] "Today I had the joy of offering Jesus many sacrifices in working to conquer my predominant fault," she wrote in her *Diary* when she was eighteen or nineteen years old. "It cost me dearly, and I recognize all my weakness.... When I receive an

---

[29] Poem 4, August 17, 1894, in *Gli Scritti*, p. 672. This is the first echo in Elizabeth's writings of St. Teresa of Ávila's maxim "Suffer or die" (cf. *Diary*, April 5, 1899).

[30] *Summarium* of the cause of Elizabeth's beatification, *Elisabetta parla ancora*, no. 13.

[31] Poem 43, December 8, 1897, in *Gli Scritti*, p. 694.

unjust criticism I can feel my blood boil in my veins and my whole being rebels!... But Jesus was with me, I could hear his voice in the depth of my heart and so I was willing to bear everything for love of him!"[32]

She consecrated herself to Mary, writing, "On every Marian feast I renew my consecration to the heavenly Mother.... Today [February 2, 1899] I entrusted my future and my vocation to her. Yes, because Jesus doesn't want me yet, His will be done, but I will grow holy in the world." And she considered herself "Jesus' bride," so closely united to Him that she could not be separated from Him, tightly bound to Him in the great work of the salvation of souls: "How I long to bring them to Jesus! I would give my life just to help ransom one of those souls that Jesus so loved. How I want to make Him known and loved in all the earth; how I would like the whole world to accept His easy yoke and His light burden."[33]

She began making small sacrifices. She read Teresa of Ávila's *Way of Perfection* with great profit to her prayer life and "to offer my will every moment of the day."[34] She attended the parish mission in Dijon in March–April 1899. In her *Diary* she took notes of the "instructions" given and recorded her personal impressions, prayers, invocations, and intentions. At the conclusion of the mission she wrote, "How I miss the mission! It was so wonderful to listen to the Word of God three times a day."[35]

That same year, Elizabeth read *The Story of a Soul* by Thérèse of Lisieux and, struck by the saint's "Offering to Merciful Love,"

---

[32] *Diary* 30, January 1899, in *Gli Scritti*, p. 519.
[33] Ibid. (The text is slightly modified.)
[34] Ibid., February 20, 1899, pp. 522–523.
[35] Ibid., April 5, 1899, p. 581.

wanted to live the same ideal. In her *Personal Notes* are expressions such as "victim-host"; and her petition "Make me a martyr of Your Love, that this martyrdom might make me die. Take away my freedom to displease You"; and "It is so beautiful to suffer for You, with You. Every beat of my heart is a cry of love and gratitude."[36]

LIFE IN THE CLOISTER

On March 26, 1899, Elizabeth received her mother's consent to enter Carmel upon turning twenty-one, that is, if she waited until 1901.

So she continued her Carmelite existence in the world. In January 1890, during a day retreat, she wrote on a piece of paper: "O Jesus ... how sweet it is to love You, to be Yours, to have You as my sole All.... Make my life a continual prayer, one long act of love. Let nothing distract me from You.... I would love to live with You in silence, O my Maestro.... I offer You the cell of my heart, so that it can be Your little Bethany. Come and rest. I love You so much.... I want to console You and I offer myself as a victim, O Maestro, for You, with You. From now on I will accept all the sacrifices, all the trials, even that of not feeling You near. I ask You only one thing, that I might always be generous and faithful."[37]

---

[36] *Personal Notes*, 4, after November 16, 1899, in *J'ai trouvé Dieu*, vol. II, p. 113.

[37] Here the influence of Thérèse of Lisieux can be seen. Elizabeth was reading the second edition of *The Story of a Soul* (Paris, 1899) when she wrote these quoted exclamations. *Personal Notes*, 5, in *J'ai trouvé Dieu*, vol. II, pp. 114–115.

From January 23 to 27, 1900, Elizabeth participated in the spiritual exercises preached by the Jesuit father Joseph Hoppenot. "Days awaited with great impatience," as she wrote in her *Diary*. "Since I cannot break from the world and live in Your solitude, allow me at least solitude of heart."

Reflecting on her social life and her numerous obligations to parties and dances, she exclaimed, "Good Maestro, You know how little joy I feel in participating in these gatherings and worldly parties. My consolation is that of recollecting myself and enjoying Your presence within me."[38] Some people, in fact, noticed that Elizabeth was not present in spirit, but only in body (as she herself confirmed). Another person, having noticed her particularly radiant look during an evening dance said, "Elizabeth isn't here: she sees God." Her reply was simply a smile. Later she would confide to Mother Germana of Jesus, "In the midst of all the parties, I was so taken up by my Maestro and by the thought of the next day's Communion that I became insensible to, estranged from, all that was happening around me."[39]

In February 1900, at the Dijon Carmel, Elizabeth met the Dominican Father Irénée Vallée,[40] prior of the convent in Dijon, spiritual director of many religious, and a famous preacher. Fr. Irénée was highly esteemed at Carmel. The sisters willingly listened to his theologically rich conferences. On this occasion, the young candidate began to speak to him of herself and of her experiences. He explained to her the mystery of the indwelling of the Trinitarian God in the soul by grace.

---

[38] *Diary* 23, January 1900, in *Gli Scritti*, p. 582.

[39] See V. Macca, *Elisabetta della Trinità: Un'esperienza di grazia nel cuore della chiesa* (Roma, 1976), p. 9.

[40] For more about Fr. Vallée see A. de Pitters, *Un grand Prêcheur: Le T. P. Vallée 1841–1927* (Paris, 1934).

Likely he began with the Pauline text, "Do you not know that you are the temple of God, and that the Spirit of God dwells in you?" (1 Cor. 3:16). The Dominican, realizing that he was speaking with someone endowed with particular graces, would later say to Mother Mary of Jesus, "This soul was ready: I told her everything at once. She took off like one crushed by the weight of the divine riches."[41]

This divine mystery was too great for Elizabeth to be satisfied with theological explanations. Both before and after entering Carmel, she met time and time again with the famous Dominican whose homilies the prioress passed along to her to read, such as the one he gave on July 16, 1900. Typical of a young person, she was influenced by the popularity of this Dominican, particularly during 1901 and 1902. She even recommended to her mother that she go to see him, because it would be good for her.[42]

Elizabeth had a good memory, and it is possible that through their conversations and his preaching she used some of Fr. Ireneo's phrases to express her own thoughts. From her studies of music, she was so used to recalling perfectly the pieces she played that it is unlikely she did not do so in other situations. The same thing happened to her in reading the writings of St. Teresa of Ávila, St. John of the Cross, and Blessed Jan Ruusbroec.

Elizabeth entered Carmel on August 2, 1901. Awaiting her was the subprioress, Mother Germana of Jesus, with some of the sisters. The prioress was absent due to the founding of the monastery at Paray-le-Monial. Elizabeth's face bore traces of the suffering she felt in leaving her mother, her sister Guite, and all that had held an interest for her.

---

[41] Macca, *Elisabetta*, p. 12.

[42] To her mother, L92, September 12, 1901, in *Gli Scritti*, p. 177.

The Discalced Carmelites first arrived in Dijon in 1602 under the guidance of the Venerable Anna of Jesus Lobera, companion of the great mystic of Ávila and spiritual daughter of John of the Cross, to found one of the first Teresian monasteries in France. In 1790 the French Revolution expelled them, and it was not until 1865 that the new monastery in rue Carnot[43] was reestablished. It soon flourished to the point of necessitating consideration of another new foundation at Paray-le-Monial.

In fact, six religious had already left when Elizabeth entered Carmel, and five more were waiting to depart. Twenty-four religious welcomed the young candidate, who was the seventh in the novitiate. She had no need to discern her religious name; she knew she was Elizabeth of the Trinity, and this name carried within itself all the aspirations of her short life as a Carmelite.[44]

Her ability to recollect herself was striking. "She saw everything in God and God in everything," someone said. "She was so absorbed in God that sometimes she got lost in the monastery."[45] Mother Germana, her teacher and future prioress recalled, "that day, August 2, 1901, the doors of Carmel opened to welcome the happy postulant; it was the first Friday of the month, a day consecrated to the pains of the Savior and to reparation, a double attraction for Elizabeth, who placed her feet inside the holy

---

[43] In 1979 the Dijon Carmelites moved to another monastery, founded at Flavignerot, on a hilltop less than two miles southeast of Dijon. All that remains of the old monastery is Elizabeth's cell, rebuilt at the new monastery.

[44] In a letter to Canon Angles dated June 14, 1901, she wrote, "Did I ever tell you my Carmelite name? 'Mary Elizabeth of the Trinity'. This name seems to indicate a particular vocation. Isn't it beautiful?"

[45] Macca, *Elisabetta*, p. 12.

monastery, where she knew the suffering heart of Jesus was honored in a particular way. There, under the grace emanating from that mystery that she already nurtured with her prayer, Elizabeth would live out her office of consoling angel until her death."[46]

IN THE SILENCE OF THE NOVITIATE

Elizabeth did not have difficulty settling in at Carmel. Everything seemed delicious, in prayer as well as in the humble tasks of daily life. "You find the Good Lord at the laundry room as well as at prayer. There is nothing but Him everywhere. You live Him, breathe Him," she wrote to her sister, describing her first wash day at Carmel.[47] In order not to get her postulant's veil wet, she put on her night cap, pulled up her long habit, covering it with a large apron, and put clogs on her feet, because the usual Carmelite shoes (made of cord and burlap) fell apart if they got wet. You can just imagine what she was able to accomplish, inexperienced as she was in doing such work. And yet she was filled with joy.

Her health held up under the austerities of monastic life. Except for the first few months, during which she needed to rest more than the others, Elizabeth was able to follow the full *horarium*. The celebration of the Divine Office in Latin, two hours of meditation, and the Eucharist, occupied six hours of her day. These

---

[46] *Reminiscences*, p. 81.
[47] To her sister, Marguerite, L89, August 30, 1901, in *Gli Scritti*, p. 171.

are the hours in which the postulant practices abandoning herself to God's love in order to receive the necessary strength to persevere in her efforts to plumb the depths of the interior abyss in recollection and not to abandon that recollection during the hours of work and recreation.

Elizabeth passed many hours in her cell, which was furnished with a hard straw cot (not without its dangers, as one can roll out on either side onto the floor), a small stool, and a bookstand on a board. She saw her cell as a "small nest, dearer than all others, similar in size to my room at home, the bed and the window in the same place, the door in place of my dresser and in the corner, where I have my washstand, a bookstand, on which I am writing you, with a copy of *The Spiritual Combat*"[48] by Lorenzo Scupoli. The white walls of the cell, adorned with a large cross of dark wood without a corpus, made the cell like a holy place. She wrote, "We are both so well here! I keep silent and listen and love Him, while the mending needle passes again and again." She found her cell full of mystery and silence, "the place where she desired to sacrifice and conform herself to the crucified Bridegroom."[49]

On October 9, Mother Mary of Jesus was named prioress of the new foundation, and Mother Germana of Jesus, only thirty-one years old, was elected to take her place. Assisting her as subprioress, Mary of the Trinity, twenty-six years old, was charged with initiating the postulants into religious life. The prioress took the formation of the novices upon herself, explaining the Rule and constitutions to them every day.

[48] To Francesca de Sourdon, L88, August 22, 1901, in *Gli Scritti*, p. 167.
[49] *Reminiscences*, p. 184.

After four months Elizabeth was admitted to take the habit on the feast of the Immaculate Conception, December 8, 1901. In the morning she put on a bridal gown and, as was the custom at the time, spent a few hours outside the cloister with her family and friends, since the ceremony of vestiture (which bestows the brown habit, a scapular, a leather belt, and the white veil of the novitiate) was scheduled for the afternoon. Mass was to be presided over by the Bishop of Dijon, Monsignor Le Nordez, and the homilist was Fr. Vallée. When Elizabeth reentered the cloister she was, according to the prioress, "raptured to the point of being completely unaware of all that happened around her."[50] Her desire was to be like the Virgin Mary, "clothed with the dear habit of Carmel."[51]

On that same day, the canonical year of her novitiate began, a year of tests of unconditional fidelity, but also a year of the dark night and of purifying darkness.

In fact, the Lord tries His favorites. Elizabeth would suffer a trial that remained hidden from her fellow sisters who were distracted by their justified fear of being expelled from France. In Paris the people were working for the separation of church and state. Since the bishop was threatened, because he caused great divisions in his diocese, the Carmelite community was thinking of taking refuge in Switzerland. In November 1902 Mother Germana took a trip to the French region of Switzerland to search for a suitable place.

Elizabeth didn't seem preoccupied with worries about the future; the younger sisters were barely aware of all the political

[50] Ibid., p. 191.
[51] She expressed this desire in a letter to Canon Angles, L99, December 1, 1901, in *Gli Scritti*, p. 184.

and diocesan happenings. For Elizabeth the novitiate year was a difficult passage through the night of purification: she suffered scruples about not living the Carmelite life well, and she experienced only dryness in prayer, interior distress, and an excessive sensitivity, which caused her suffering for every least thing.

The life of pure faith that she had begun to experience before her entrance to Carmel was realized almost cruelly in her. "There is no longer a veil to hide Him (the Divine Bridegroom) from me," she wrote to her sister, Marguerite, in her suffering, "but a thick wall. It's hard, don't you think, after having felt Him so near?" These are the signs of divine favor: to take part in His agony, to drink with Him from the bitter chalice. But Elizabeth declares herself "willing to remain in this state as long as it pleases my Beloved to leave me here, because my faith tells me that He is still there and always will be." She forced herself to overcome her anxieties and her interior distress by faith, which was everything. "What are sweetness and consolations for, if not for Him?... Let's go to Him by pure faith."[52]

There is no other written record of Elizabeth's interior sufferings during her novitiate year.

She confided only in Mother Germana, a highly gifted teacher who fully and faithfully followed St. Teresa of Ávila's recommendations to the prioress: try to be loved so that you might be obeyed. The sole witness of Elizabeth's difficult journey through the novitiate, Mother Germana, noted that Elizabeth "heroically committed to living her faith in God's presence, in the depth of her soul." Mother Germana intuited this was the work of God, who demolishes the old man to build the new, transforming him by pain. "It was her sanctification and, I would

---

[52] To Marguerite Gollot, L53, May 8, 1901, in *Gli Scritti*, p. 125.

say, her martyrdom. I remember that one day she said to me: 'The Lord doesn't want me to have a single thought outside of Him, and yet He is so hidden that it's as if He didn't exist. He really expects heroism.'"[53]

Rare were the moments of consolation that interrupted her painful novitiate year. In October, during the spiritual exercises preached by Fr. Vallée, Elizabeth, in great agony because of the darkness in her soul, went to him in the hope of receiving his help and counsel. He did not understand her. He saw a change, yes, but this young woman with an expression of great distress on her face left him feeling disconcerted. "You have changed my Elizabeth," he said to the prioress, asking her not to send Elizabeth to him anymore. The novice was left to dwell alone "at the foot of the cross, remaining silent before the crucifix listening, thus penetrating all its secrets."[54]

In the midst of this night of the spirit, Elizabeth had to ask herself if she had the strength to pronounce her vows and chain herself forever to Carmel. The community admitted her to the Profession: the novice's behavior left no doubt about her suitability. The sisters knew nothing of the shadows and interior struggles, which lasted until the vigil of her Profession. Only after a meeting with a prudent and expert religious was Elizabeth able to overcome them. ·

On January 11, 1903, Elizabeth was consecrated forever to the Lord. In the chapter hall of the monastery, in the presence of the entire community, Elizabeth was "captivated by the thought of immolation expressed in the reading in Vespers from that day: 'I appeal to you therefore brethren, by the mercies of God, to

---

[53] Macca, *Elisabetta*, p. 13.
[54] To her sister, Marguerite, L158, June 2, 1901, in *Gli Scritti*, p. 130.

present your bodies as a living sacrifice, holy and acceptable to God' (Rom. 12:1)." Mother Germana commented, "This was the spirit with which she made her vows of poverty, chastity, and obedience, which consecrated her forever as a bride of Christ."[55]

SPOUSE OF CHRIST

The first letter written by Elizabeth after her Profession was to her Rolland aunts, expressing the happiness of her soul. "I would like to speak to you about my Profession, but you see, it was something so divine that earthly language is powerless to say it." She explained that it was absolutely different from every other day of her life, "a day without sunset ... the beginning of the day that never ends."[56]

Now all her hopes had been realized. She was Christ's bride. She passed many hours in adoration of the mystery of her Three. Now all was accepted: the pains, the desire; in the shadow of the new light that illuminated her soul, she felt a progressive transformation brought about by living and suffering as Christ's bride.

To be Christ's bride!

It is not simply the expression of the sweetest dream: it is a divine reality; the expression of a whole mystery of likeness and union.... It is to be sacrificed like Him, for Him, by means of Him.... It is to rest in Him and allow Him to rest in her.

---

[55] *Reminiscences*, p. 101.
[56] To her Rolland aunts, L154, ca. January 12, 1903, in *Gli Scritti*, pp. 236–237.

Elizabeth thinks of Mary Magdalene, who offers Jesus her house in Bethany to rest, and Elizabeth wants to become a small Bethany and so enjoy divine intimacy. For Elizabeth, to be Christ's bride means to "enter into all His joys, participate in all His sufferings. It is to be abundantly fruitful, co-redemptrix, to birth souls to grace, multiply the adopted children of the Father, the redeemed of Christ, co-heirs of His glory." To be a bride of Christ at Carmel requires "Elijah's heart of fire and the pierced heart of Teresa—his 'true bride', to be zealous for His glory." (This alludes to the first antiphon from Vespers on the saint's feast day.)

To be a spouse of Christ is to be chosen as a "mystical bride, to have enraptured His heart to the point of overcoming every separation, [so that] the Word might pour out into the soul as it does in the breast of the Father, with the same ecstatic love!" Elizabeth contemplates the Father, the Word, and the Spirit who invade the soul, divinize it, and consummate it in love in the One. Behold the wedding, the marriage, the indissoluble union of wills and hearts. "And God says: 'Let us make a bride, fitting for him. They will be two in one" (This is an allusion to Genesis 2:18, 24).

In developing these thoughts, recorded in her *Personal Notes*, this Carmelite ideal took hold of her and captivated her: "The Carmelite is a sacrament of Christ. In her everything must radiate (Fr. Donner) our holy God, the God who was crucified for love. In order to radiate Him, it is necessary that she allow herself to be transformed into His very image and likeness, possessing a faith that prays without interruption; a will imprisoned in His, which never distances itself from His; a true heart, that is, pure; and that she tremble under the blessing of the Master."[57]

---

[57] *Personal Notes*, 13, ca. mid-1902, and 14, ca. mid-1903, in *Gli Scritti*, pp. 122–123, 124–125.

The adventure of her attempt to live up to this ideal is re-counted in her letters and poems. And although never perfectly achieved, she remained committed until her death.

Five or six months after her Profession, the first symptoms of her illness manifested themselves; it was Addison's disease, an unknown and therefore untreatable endocrine disorder. Ex-haustion, stomach cramps, strong migraines, and weight loss were her symptoms. She tried to hide her sickness and asked to continue living the Rule's horarium and abstinences, but, in the evening after Matins, at around eleven o'clock, going back to her cell, she was so exhausted that she would be forced to crawl up the stairs. She carried on like this for two years, hid-ing her symptoms in silence. During these years she preferred to read from John of the Cross's writings, particularly *Spiritual Canticle* and *The Living Flame of Love*, from which she received the strength to bear her pains without complaint and to con-tinue her regular work.

At the beginning of 1906, she could no longer hide her atro-cious pains and in particular the horrific attacks of stomach pain. An ulcer was suspected, or tuberculosis; how ought she be cared for? Her pain kept her from eating. She could tolerate only a little milk, taken one drop at a time; this was her diet. If she ate something "in obedience," she vomited it up immediately. She was transferred to the infirmary and from March 20, 1906, her bed became the altar on which Elizabeth's sacrifice was slowly consumed. "May my very self be distilled drop by drop for His glory," was one of her last thoughts, recorded on a small scrap of paper.

In July 1906, in a letter to Canon Angles she shared, "If you knew what work of destruction I feel in my whole being! It is the way of Calvary that has opened, and I am so very happy to walk it as a bride next to the divine Crucified." Aware that she would die that same year, she asked to be "consecrated, during Mass, like a victim-host of praise to God's glory," so that, "the Father, looking at me," no longer sees Elizabeth, but "may recognize Him [Christ]; and that 'I am conformed to His death,' that I suffer in my body that which was lacking in His Passion for His body the Church."[58]

In her final letters, tirelessly recorded in pencil with trembling hand, Elizabeth's thought reaches the summit of her earthly sojourn. Reading some of her typical expressions, one cannot help but be convinced that she was a Carmelite gifted with authentic mystical experiences.

Hers is a love purified by profound, ardent suffering, which desires to be conformed to the image of Christ, the Son of God, crucified to redeem fallen humanity. It is a love raised in offering to God, as is revealed in her "Hymn to the Trinity," which she composed in 1904 (O my God, Trinity whom I adore . . .[59]).

As a novice Elizabeth had discovered her vocation to exist solely for the praise of the glory of God, to adore Him in that heaven of her soul where He lives. Here at the twilight of her life, that vocation becomes the song of a heart burdened with unbearable sufferings, but strong in its desire to offer itself for the Bridegroom.

> A praise of glory is a soul of silence that remains like a lyre under the mysterious touch of the Holy Spirit so that He may draw from it divine harmonies; it knows

---

[58] To Canon Angles, L294, July 8 or 9, 1906, in *Gli Scritti*, pp. 433–434.

[59] The prayer appears on pages 44–45.

that suffering is a string that produces still more beautiful sounds; so it loves to see this string on its instrument that it may more delightfully move the Heart of its God.[60]

In the final months of her life Elizabeth prayerfully composed two cycles of meditations based on numerous biblical passages and with references to other works (the fruit of her own long meditations on them): *Heaven in Faith* (July 1906) and the *Last Retreat* (August 1906). At the same time she composed a letter in the form of a spiritual treatise to Francis de Sourdon on *The Greatness of Our Vocation* (September 1906). Finally, she wrote *Let Yourself Be Loved* (October 1906), a last note to her prioress, Germana of Jesus, drafted toward the end of October,[61] to be read when "the little Praise of Glory will no longer sing on earth, but will live in the immense furnace of love."

She lived out her final days with great courage, allowing herself to be crucified by Love and waiting to meet the Bridegroom. October 29, she saw her mother, her sister, and her two nieces for the last time. From behind the grille Elizabeth gave her blessing to the girls. With the presentiment of never seeing her mother again, she said, "Mother, when our extern sister comes to tell you that I have finished suffering, drop to your knees, saying, 'My God, You gave her to me, and I return her to You. Blessed be Your

---

[60] *Heaven in Faith*, 10.2, in *Gli Scritti*, p. 631. The image of the lyre, taken from St. Thérèse — in her breviary Elizabeth had a holy card of St. Thérèse with a lyre in her hands — is mentioned three times in *Last Retreat*, in three letters written during the summer of 1906 and in her poems. Thanks to her musical formation the image of the harp particularly captivated her imagination.

[61] *Let Yourself Be Loved*, in *J'ai trouvé Dieu*, vol. Ia, pp. 196–199.

holy Name.' "[62] And trying to disguise her sadness, she returned to her painful "prison" "to prepare for eternal life," entrusting herself to Mary Immaculate (*Janua Coeli*).[63]

With the words "I go to Light, to Love, to Life," whispered as the final song of Laudem Gloriae, the Carmelite of Dijon died on November 9, 1906. (Perhaps these very words, used by Gustav Mahler in one of his greatest musical compositions, were familiar to her.) A fellow sister recounted seeing Elizabeth, "sitting on the bed, her eyes fixed in front of her. Her eyes remained so until her last breath, at least a quarter of an hour, not in an ecstatic expression, but with a natural face, and not that of a sick person either, but with her eyes fixed upward on a fairly high point. At a certain moment she hiccupped. It was done.... Her eyes remained so beautiful."[64]

The process for her beatification, introduced in 1931, was not completed until 1987. But her mission to bring souls to God through interior recollection in the depths of their own souls continues today, in these times that are profoundly marked by the search for a new hope and a rediscovery of values such as silence, prayer, and solitude.[65]

---

[62] Deposition of Mrs. Catez at the process of beatification; cf. *Reminiscences*, p. 205.

[63] To Canon Angles, L294, July 8 or 9, 1906, in *Gli Scritti*, p. 434.

[64] Cf. M. Philipon, *L'inabitazione della Trinità nell'anima* (Milano, 1966), p. 237.

[65] In March 2016 Pope Francis advanced the cause of Blessed Elizabeth of the Trinity for canonization. —Trans.

CHAPTER TWO

BETWEEN EXISTENCE AND DOCTRINE

A Lived Spirituality

Elizabeth of the Trinity crossed the threshold of the Dijon Carmel aware that she was embracing a life that, by vocation and mission, had prayer, silence, solitude, and an unceasing conversation with God at its center. She felt called to consecrate her entire existence to a living relationship with God-Trinity, with Christ, as an expression of a love that desires to be, in the words of St. Thérèse, "a lifting of the heart, a simple glance to heaven, a cry of gratitude and love amidst trials and joy."[66]

Her sense of the call to consecrate her entire existence highlights the fact that, for Elizabeth, life and doctrine, experience and writings, combine and complete each other, each one enlightening the other. With the clarity of that enlightenment the great themes of her lived spirituality can be understood: the presence of the Trinity within her being, conformity to Christ,

---

[66] Thérèse of the Child Jesus, *Autobiographical Writings* C, 317, in *Gli Scritti*, p. 289.

the making of her existence into a praise of the glory of God: all of these unified and ordered toward a deeply lived life of faith.

Elizabeth wrote about this in her writings, letters, and spontaneous poems, revealing her most intimate thoughts without any intention of presenting any "doctrine." From these documents the sources and influences on her thought can be seen, especially from her reading of Teresa of Ávila's *Way of Perfection* and the works of Thérèse of Lisieux and John of the Cross and, more generally, through the great mission held at Dijon and the retreats preached by Fr. Vallée. Nevertheless, her primary inspiration is the Holy Spirit. Her interior progress and the illuminations that follow explain, first of all, that it is the Holy Spirit who is "the true interior teacher of Elizabeth," a fact highlighted during the process of her beatification.[67]

Perhaps the young Elizabeth did not yet grasp with the inspiration of the Holy Spirit that mysterious source of light and love that enabled her to discover God's presence within herself and that allowed her to live that presence as a gift in harmony with her whole being. Only as she matured did she perceive the action of the Holy Spirit in her soul. And only then did she understand that from her childhood the Spirit had directed her, visiting her in the depths of a lived faith.

In a letter, she defined her interior attitude, writing, "The plan for my retreat will be to hold myself in faith and love under the 'anointing of the Holy [Spirit],' of whom St. John writes, because He alone 'penetrates the depths of God.' Pray that I do not cause Him sorrow, this Spirit of love, but rather that I allow Him to effect in me all the works of His grace."[68]

---

[67] Macca, *Elisabetta*, p. 26.
[68] To Canon Angles, L230, June 1, 1905, in *Gli Scritti*, p. 348.

This plan, begun many years earlier, guided her in her ascetical practices and above all toward a wisdom-filled understanding of the Scriptures.

Elizabeth, gifted with a particularly sensitive musical intuition, and used to losing herself in the melodies of the pieces she played on the piano, had no difficulty going beyond the visible world to attend to the interior voice of the Spirit. She felt as though she were penetrated by a presence, by a reality that she understood only in light of God's Word.

This presence opened her spirit, enriching it with a sense of healthy balance, to love life and open itself to the beauty of creation. Yet at the same time it pushed her to consider her life in light of the apostle Paul's words: to exist for the praise of the glory of God, "for from him and through him and to him are all things. To him be glory for ever. Amen" (Rom. 11:36) and to offer a "spiritual worship" to God by making herself "a living sacrifice" (Rom. 12:1).

THE TRINITARIAN INDWELLING

Elizabeth's spiritual journey highlighted the mystery of the Trinity, present by grace in the soul of every baptized person. Her name tells her she is the "house of God" in which live the Three Divine Persons: the Father, the Son, and the Holy Spirit. The connection between her vocation and her name, more than simply the fruit of her own reflections, is strengthened in the successive layers of her life's experiences, and consequently deeper meanings of her first intuition are revealed. At first Elizabeth thinks only of the gospel mystery of the indwelling of God through grace and the ensuing intimacy enjoyed by the soul, of the "little heaven" that we have within us, as she learned from St. Teresa of Ávila. Later this truth about her name will bring a vertical dimension to her spirituality; she wants to live in adoration of the mystery of the Trinity, contemplating God's presence to the point of losing herself in God as in a deep abyss. "I so love this mystery of the Holy Trinity," she writes to Canon Angles. "It is an abyss in which I lose myself."[69]

For Elizabeth the adoration of the Trinity in the soul makes earthly life something sublime, capable of conferring unhoped-for experiences of that intimate love that forgets itself and exists solely for the other. "Dear little sister," she exclaims in a letter, "let us lose ourselves in this Holy Trinity, in the God-All-Love; let us allow ourselves to be carried away to that place where there is nothing but Him, Him alone!"[70]

These words were written two months before she entered Carmel. And to emphasize that God lives in us and allows us to unite our lives to His in inexplicable but real ways, this future Carmelite wrote on the back of a holy card to her sister, "May the 'One' be realized" — you could say the Unity-of-Love — "in our souls with the Father, the Son, and the Holy Spirit." It seems, in fact, that Elizabeth considered herself a "bride of the Trinity."[71]

---

[69] To Canon Angles, L62, June 14, 1901, in *Gli Scritti*, p. 136.

[70] To Marguerite Gollot, L58, June 2, 1901, in *Gli Scritti*, p. 130.

[71] L59, June 2, 1901, *J'ai trouvé Dieu*, vol. II, p. 228. See also the note written on the back of a holy card for Sr. Mary of the Trinity dated May 25 (1902?), L114: "Que l'*Un* se consumme au plus profond de nos âmes avec le Père, le Fils et le Saint-Esprit" (May the *One* be realized in our souls with the Father, the Son, and the Holy Spirit) (*J'ai trouvé Dieu*, vol. Ib, p. 83) and the note written underneath St. Catherine of Siena's Prayer to the Trinity: "Que les Tres fondent nos âmes dans l'unité d'une même foi et d'un même amour" (May the Three unite our souls

This can be inferred from a poem written at Pentecost 1898. In the final line she implores the Holy Spirit to consume her in the divine flames:

> This spouse [of] the Trinity
> Who desires naught but His will …[72]

It is true, these are only the first mentions of that sublime mystery that intensified after her entrance at Carmel and that finds its highest expression in her well-known prayer to the Trinity. But something that was already stirring explodes within her in 1902 when the novices celebrated the feast of the Most Holy Trinity for the first time in Carmel. On that day, which was also the name day of the novices' "angel," Sr. Mary of the Trinity, Elizabeth presented her with a semiautobiographical poem that revealed her fervent heart. The bride of the Trinity par excellence is certainly the Virgin Mary, but at Carmel there lived another virgin, Sr. Mary of the Trinity, upon whom Elizabeth transferred her intimate sentiments:

> On the mountain of Carmel lives another Mary,
> in intimate union with God, all-pervaded by Him,
> in a recollection interior and mysterious,
> all to her God given over,
> night and day ceaselessly.[73]

That same day, writing to her sister, Marguerite, Elizabeth shared her joy at having celebrated the feast in the depths of

---

in the oneness of the same faith and the same love) (unknown recipient).

[72] Poem 54, May 29, 1898, *J'ai trouvé Dieu*, vol. II, p. 113, *Gli Scritti*, p. 708 (text slightly modified).

[73] Poem 78, May 25, 1902, in *Gli Scritti*, pp. 742–743.

her soul. "Oh yes, my dear Guite, this feast of the Three is truly my feast; for me there is none other like it." These words seem to recall a mystical-spousal experience. She explains, "The feast was good at Carmel because it is a feast of silence and adoration. Never have I understood so well the mystery and the entire vocation that there is in my name."[74]

Days of intense meditation and adoration of the mystery of the "Three" followed and blossomed into this poem, which was written in celebration of the prioress and would have been sung during recreation to the melody of "Reste avec moi, Jesus-Eucharistie":

> In the bosom of the Three, flooded with light,
> with the splendors of God's countenance,
> we penetrate the secret of the mystery
> which every day appears more radiant.
> To be infinite, unfathomable depth,
> We communicate with You, Divinity.
> O Trinity, O God, our unchanging,
> we see You, You Yourself, in Your lucidity.[75]

The adoration of the mystery of the Trinitarian indwelling invites Elizabeth to lose herself in praise. From the beginning of 1904, the great Pauline hymn in Ephesians 1:3–12 had struck a chord in the depths of her soul: to live *in laudem gloriae gratiae suae*.

"I want to share an intimate secret," she would write after almost two years of intensely living this Pauline teaching. "My dream is to be 'the praise of His glory.' I read it in St. Paul, and

---

[74] Letter to her sister, Marguerite, L113, May 25, 1902, in *Gli Scritti*, p. 200.

[75] Poem 80, in *Gli Scritti*, p. 744 (Italian translation corrected).

my Spouse let me understand that since the beginning of my exile this has been my vocation, while I wait to go sing the eternal *Sanctus* in the city of the Saints."[76] But singing the glory of God is for Elizabeth intoning a song raised to her Three, a resounding *Sanctus* that extends on in praise of the God-Trinity.

Here it is important to recall the historic moment in which Elizabeth formulated in a letter to her family friend Canon Angles her proposal to draw near to the immensity of God in Three Persons through an attitude of praise. The year was 1905.

On December 9 of that same year, the French Republic had promulgated a law mandating the separation of church and state. It was published on December 11 in the *Journal officiel*. On December 29 an administrative decree concerning the inventory of the Church's goods was published, ignoring Pope Pius X's previously published encyclical in which he gave a clear call to *establish all things in Christ*. This work was well known to Elizabeth, and she recognized it as an invitation to make the pope's program her own. In fact, Elizabeth's aforementioned letter begins by repeating the motto from the encyclical and adds, "How we feel the need to be made holy, to forget ourselves so as to give ourselves totally to the interests of the Church.... Poor France! I would like to cover her with the blood of the Just One, of Him who lives eternally to make intercession and beg for mercy. How sublime is the Carmelite's mission; she must be a mediator with Jesus Christ."[77]

In Elizabeth's thought, this was simply part of being a *Praise of God*. Aware of being *laudem gloriae* (which she adopted as

---

[76] To Canon Angles, L256, end of December 1905, *J'ai trouvé Dieu*, vol. Ib, p. 326. (This letter is missing from the Italian translation cited.)

[77] Ibid., p. 327; allusion to Heb. 7:25 and 4:16.

her name toward the end of her life), identifying herself with Christ in the Passion, she was transformed in Christ and became a mediator with Him. Her favorite song—the praise of the glory—thus became the fulfillment of the economy of grace: *to restore all things in Christ* (cf. Eph. 1:10).

This ideal of adoration and praise of the Trinity is summed up in her prayer O *my God, Trinity Whom I adore*, of November 21, 1904, truly one of the most beautiful prayers ever composed in the history of the Church.

O my God, Trinity whom I adore, help me to forget myself entirely, and establish me in You, calm and quiet as though my soul were already in eternity; that nothing might disturb my peace or cause me to leave You, my Unchanging Good, but that every moment You draw me ever deeper into the depths of Your mystery. Quiet my soul, make it Your heaven, Your favorite dwelling, and Your resting place; may I never leave You alone, but be wholly present, entirely vigilant in my faith, wholly adoring, wholly abandoned to Your creative action.

O my Beloved Christ, crucified for love, I want to be the bride of Your Heart, I want to cover You with glory, I want to love You ... to the point of dying of love! ... But I feel my impotence, and I ask You to clothe me with Yourself, to identify my soul with every movement of Your Soul, to drown me, invade me, substitute Yourself for me, so that my life may be nothing more than an effusion of Your life. Come into my soul as Adorer, as "Reparator," and as Savior. O Eternal Word, Word of my God, I want to spend my life listening to You, I want to become docility itself so as to learn all things from You. Then, through all the nights,

*all the emptiness, all powerlessness, I want to fix my gaze
on You and remain in Your great light. O my Beloved Star,
enchant me so that I can no longer leave the splendor of
Your rays.*

*O consuming Fire, Spirit of love, come over me so that
in my soul there is an incarnation of the Word so that I might
be for Him an extra-added humanity in whom He can renew
all His mystery; and You, O Father, bend down to Your little
creature, cover her with Your shadow, and see in her only
Your Beloved in whom You have placed all Your delight.*

*O my Three, my All, my Blessedness, Infinite Solitude,
Immensity in Whom I lose myself, I hand myself over to
You as Your prey. Bury Yourselves in me so that I may be
buried in You, while I await coming to contemplate by Your
light, the abyss of Your greatness.*

In the first and final parts of this prayer Elizabeth cancels
and sets aside time in order to bury herself in adoration of the
Trinity. The second and the third parts recall her Christocentric
spirituality and her openness to the Holy Spirit—Consuming
Fire, Light, and Love.

Conformity to Christ

The Carmelite of Dijon composed her famous prayer to the Trinity under the influence of the Holy Spirit. He is a presence that
suddenly breaks into her existence and touches her profoundly.
This melody expressed as a prayer constitutes the synthesis of her
doctrine. It reveals to us how her love for God made adoration
and praise a no-longer-belonging-to-herself; the birth of her destiny to conformity with Christ Crucified; and the recognition of

the allure of silence as the vital atmosphere of her own existence; it is to read in the darkness of faith the signs of a Presence that radiates light, that illuminates the darkness of the night.

Her earlier efforts to believe in God's presence in the heaven of her heart, at a time when everything seemed covered in deep shadows, and the fixing of her gaze toward the contemplation of God-Trinity, from whom all are descended, had prepared in her that profound love that now enkindled that mysterious encounter with the Three. This encounter gave rise to a new awareness of the themes that later became hallmarks of her interior life. One could say that Elizabeth wrote this prayer in order to manifest her own change. With a few well-chosen words she expressed, acknowledged, and sang of the transformation of grace that had pervaded her entire life.

It is not that by way of intelligence and reflection she had come to grow into sublime intimacy with God. She received, welcomed, heard, and responded—loving, giving herself unconditionally, passionately repeating the "Come!" of the bride in the Song of Songs. She asked to be loved, that the Eternal Love might compose and arrange in her the entirety of her existence, open and available, humbly placed in the hands of God. All of this was realized in Christ, with Christ, for Christ "crucified for love."

In the second part of "O My God, Trinity Whom I Adore," Elizabeth entered into the mystery of the Incarnate Word. Her journey toward immersion in the Trinitarian presence was unthinkable without Jesus Christ, into whom we are grafted through Baptism (cf. Rom. 11).

Her love of the great gift of Baptism has already been noted. "Elizabeth is a baptismal soul. She understands and lives fully the promises of this sacrament, announcing those promises with astounding theological certainty and with a remarkable liturgical sense.[78] Having become the adopted daughter of the Father, "predestined to radiate the glory of His grace,"[79] she desired to live fully conformed to Christ, making her love fruitful in Him.

Even before she entered Carmel, her writings and poems manifested her spiritual program. "How sweet it is to love You, Jesus my delight, to belong to You, to have You as my sole All! Since You come to me in my heart every day [an allusion to the permission she was given to receive Communion every day], our union is even more intimate. May my life be a continuous prayer, one long act of love. May nothing draw me away from You, neither noise nor distractions.... For love of You I place myself under You with all my heart. I offer You the cell of my heart as Your little Bethany.... Every beat of my heart is an act of love. My Jesus, my God, how wonderful it is to love You, to be totally Yours!"[80]

Similar effusions occupied the pages of her *Personal Notes* for all of 1900. Following a Eucharistic experience, but before knowing of Thérèse of Lisieux's Offering, her heart was set aflame with the desire to suffer for Jesus and with Jesus, to hug the cross as a sign of love for God.

Even beyond the influence of the popular catechesis of her day, which proposed to the faithful the idea of sharing Christ's sufferings, Elizabeth's mind was imprinted with the image of

---

[78] Macca, *Elisabetta*, p. 31. In *Heaven in Faith* 1.1, Elizabeth refers to Romans to highlight the fact that in Baptism "we are grafted into Christ" (*Gli Scritti*, p. 609).

[79] To her sister, Marguerite, L239, August 1905, in *Gli Scritti*, p. 370.

[80] *Personal Notes*, in *J'ai trouvé Dieu*, vol. 2, p. 115. Probably written circa January 23, 1900.

the Beloved hanging on the tree of the Cross. Returning home after an hour of adoration during which she offered herself "as victim in union with the Crucified for the return of sinners to God," she made Teresa of Ávila's yearning, "Either die or suffer," her own, writing:

> I come to draw strength and courage,
> and to ask for the cross as an inheritance.
> Since I thirst to suffer,
> to die under the cross.
> Yes, the cross, I want it as my legacy,
> that cross tenderly loved by my God,
> upon which He died for us all.
> O Holy Cross, supreme treasure
> which Jesus gives to all those who love Him.[81]

A few days later, on the feast of the Sacred Heart, her dialogue with the Lord became a hymn in which she resolved to live a steadfast contemplation of the love of Jesus, received and perceived in the expressions given to her through grace. Previously Elizabeth had called Christ "Maestro." In this poem she uses another form characteristic of her writings, the heart as symbol of "all Love," of Him who is All-Love.

> O Sacred Heart of my Savior,
> You whom I adore, You whom I love,
> You, all Love, supreme Good,
> You alone possess my heart.

And she adds:

---

[81] Poem 55, June 1898. Italian translation in *Gli Scritti*, p. 709, corrected to reflect the original French text.

The sweetest longing of my heart
is to share suffering with You....
I desire it greatly, O Sweet Savior,
and I will find my delight
in consoling Your divine Heart
and in drinking with You the chalice [of the Passion].
I want to drink it to the dregs
as on the evening of Your agony,
reliving, my sweet Savior,
all of Your pains.

In conclusion Elizabeth explodes with an uncontrollable desire
to conform herself to Christ:

Behold my most burning desire,
my most intimate vow:
to live, to suffer, to die
and to offer myself as victim
for the love, glory, and honor
of my Delight (Beloved), of the Sacred Heart.[82]

All these desires make their way into her prayer to the Trinity:
"O my *Beloved Christ, crucified* for *love*, I want to be the *bride* of
Your *Heart*, I want to cover You with *glory*, I want to *love You* ...
until it *kills me*." That which is most striking in the words of the
young Elizabeth is certainly her enthusiasm, the vertical surg-
ing of a pure heart freed from all negative interference. But her
willingness to live her ideals and to share the cross with Jesus
even in the deep shadows of trials, when her way was shrouded

---

[82] Poem 57, feast of the Sacred Heart, June 17, 1898, in *Gli Scritti*,
pp. 170–172.

by heavy fog and she clung only to faith in the foreboding of her impending death must also be highlighted.

Here another aspect must be introduced, her certainty of faith, matured at the school of John of the Cross, that only Christ could sustain her in her intentions, her intimate desires. "I feel my impotence," she confesses. From this realization blooms her great yearning to disappear in Christ, to be clothed with Him; to give over her very life, abandoning it in Him, to become a radiating of His life. "It seems to me that the saints are souls who at every moment forget themselves; they lose themselves so completely in Him whom they love, that without returning to themselves, without creaturely regret, they can say with St. Paul, 'it is no longer I who live, but Christ who lives in me' [Gal. 2:20]. In order to arrive at this transformation one must without a doubt offer himself as a victim."[83]

The "*vivit in me Christus*" (Gal. 2:20) that she experienced while listening to the Word and the powerful transformative action of the Holy Spirit that held her in His grip coincide in Elizabeth with the affirmation of her longing to be for Christ "an extra-added humanity, in which He can renew all His mystery" as Adorer of the Father, as Reparator of the sins of a world distant from the faith, and as Savior cruelly killed on Calvary.

These are not pet images or dreams that clothe the existence of a Carmelite monastic, nor are they simply echoes of her uncontainable love for Christ-All-Love, who destroyed her fragile health in the divine flames. They are real experiences, come about in the depths of the soul, where a voice whispers: "Die every day" (1 Cor. 15:31).

---

[83] To Germana de Gemeaux L179, September 20, 1903, in *J'ai trouvé Dieu*, vol. Ib, pp.187–189 (*Gli Scritti*, p. 273).

I diminish; I renounce myself more each day so that Christ grows and is exalted in me.... I place the joy of my soul (as far as I will it, not as far as I feel) in all that which can sacrifice me, destroy me, lower me, because I want to make way for my Maestro.... I don't want to live my own life, but to be transformed into Jesus Christ so that my life is more divine than human and the Father, bending low over me, may recognize in me the image of His Beloved Son.[84]

Elizabeth outlined these thoughts at the end of her life, almost as if to gather the fruits of the steadfast commitment of her final years to order the events of her Carmelite existence according to the great Pauline themes. As a matter of fact, it was beginning in 1903 that the apostle guided her with exhortations and Christological texts toward complete conformity with Christ on Calvary. There she finds the strength to bear atrocious pains without complaint. "I never met a soul that overcame pain with such serenity, without caving in on itself, in all and through all preoccupied with the presence of God and with her own vocation as 'praise of glory.'"[85] Fr. Michel Philipon, the most famous expert on the life in the Dijon Carmel, left this declaration as his conclusion to the exhaustive examination of the "heroic virtues" of the saint, basing it on the testimonies of her contemporaries.

Here we need to consider the final pages of Elizabeth's earthly adventure, beginning with Palm Sunday 1906, when an acute episode threatened her life. In that moment, the nearness of

---

[84] Heaven in Faith, 3.2, *Gli Scritti*, pp. 613–614.
[85] *Summarium*, 702, p. 357, in Macca, *Elisabetta*, p. 47.

death, so long desired, became a moment of ecstasy. She was disappointed not to have flown to heaven, and she didn't hide that fact from her mother.[86] Writing to a friend, she spoke of the joy she felt "at the thought of her first face-to-face encounter with Divine Beauty. Oh, if only I had gone to lose myself in Him!"[87] And in another place, she again remarked about the happiness of "the indescribable days spent waiting for the great vision [of light]."[88] She continued to hope she would go soon, but the sound methods of God would make her wait five more months, comparable to a slow death. It was five months of a final purification to dissolve all the doubts that remained in her, all the imperfections in her burning desire. And what she had to say about death became more painful, more filled with suffering, because death is not a joyful mystery. Elizabeth had to convince her very own flesh to "be conformed to Christ in His death" (cf. Phil. 3:10).

This change in Elizabeth struck the noted Swiss theologian Hans Urs von Balthasar, who arrived at this conclusion: "The tendency toward the afterlife and the accentuated desire to not establish herself permanently here below, to live on earth as if on tip toes, preferring to stay suspended in the air above the ground, is a behavior which should not be ascribed to 'grace,' because it is founded in 'nature', and at first it is indifferent to grace and the demands of grace, if not diametrically opposed to it. Christianity is neither a flight from the world nor an annoyed submission to

---

[86] Cf. letter to her mother, L267, ca. April 19, 1906, in *Gli Scritti*, pp. 399.

[87] To Francesca de Sourdon, L270, end of April 1906, in *Gli Scritti*, pp. 402–403.

[88] To Germana de Gemeaux, L278, June 10, 1906, in *Gli Scritti*, p. 409.

it." Consequently, at least so it seems to von Balthasar, "Elizabeth during her final sufferings finds the way of perfect indifference with much less ease than St. Thérèse [of Lisieux]. She wants to die with every fiber of her being; she fights to fade away and to be with Christ — away from everything, and headlong down into the boundless abyss of God. She sees her apostolate is to infect as many as possible with her ardent hope for the infinite. It is a behavior that we cannot completely fathom."[89]

This truly was the predicament of Elizabeth's life, but von Balthasar fails to see how grace intervened and was victorious over the inclinations of her "nature" — a term that seems poorly chosen because in her everything is born and develops within the scope of prayer, and even more so because her nature is strongly gifted with sensibility, affection, and intuition.

In any case, Elizabeth needs to be overcome, like all Christians, by the overwhelming anguish of death, by the emptiness that rules a condition of destruction. In fact, toward the beginning of September 1906, two months before the arrival of the Beloved Bridegroom, she was able to recognize that finding herself in "extreme weakness" she had truly succeeded in "completing in [her] flesh that which lacks in the sufferings of Jesus Christ for His body which is the Church" (cf. Col. 1:24). No less was her silent joy at being chosen by God "to join with the sufferings of her Christ," but at the same time she realized in her prostrated state and continual pains that she must believe with humility and preserve her hope until that day in which the Lord would say to her, "Come." "Have you ever seen one of the holy cards that represent death in the act of cutting the sheaf in two with

---

[89] Hans Urs von Balthasar, *Sisters in Spirit*, pp. 267–269, in Italian version.

his sickle?" she wrote in a long letter, which is a short tract on the greatness of her vocation. "Well, that is my condition. I seem only to feel a little bit of death's destruction.... For nature it is sometimes distressing, and I promise that if I remained here I would feel nothing but my vileness in suffering. That is what my human eyes see." Then, repeating Catherine of Siena's formula, she affirms, "Soon, 'I will open the eye of my soul to the light of faith' and faith tells me that it is love that destroys me, that slowly consumes me."[90]

Herein lies the whole of the experience of dying without sensible consolations, the experience of the Divine Reaper, who with the sickle cuts the final fragile hostilities of the human heart so that it clings to Him alone with naked faith. In her painful journey she arrived at full conformity with Christ dead on the Cross, her poor little straw cot in the monastery's infirmary having become the cross on which she stretched out her arms to allow them to be nailed. "God so loved pain's company that He chose it for His Son, and His Son lay down on this bed, and He concurred with the Father in this love."[91] This being conformed to Him and following Him in the work of redemption is accomplished beyond the realm of the sensible, beyond natural feelings. "I cannot say I love to suffer in and of itself," she said to her mother, "but I love it because it makes me like Him who is my Bridegroom, my Love."[92] And she felt sure that the Father would find in her "the image of His Crucified Son."

[90] *The Greatness of Our Vocation, J'ai trouvé Dieu,* vol. Ia, p. 136, no. 7.
[91] Anonymous citation in a letter to Mdme. Gout de Bize, L318, September 30, 1906, in *Gli Scritti,* p. 468.
[92] To her mother, L317, October 1906, in *Gli Scritti,* pp. 475–476.

Praise of Glory

Elizabeth spoke of a second vocation, that of being praise of His glory. Only now, however, did she understand what a total identification with Jesus Christ demands. In order to become *laus gloriae* she needed to consecrate herself to God as "a victim-host of praise to His glory, so that all hopes, every movement, every act are a homage made to His holiness."[93]

Ever since reading Ephesians 1:3-12, Elizabeth continued to live in the light of this beloved formula, personalizing it as her "new name."[94] This intuition, which sums up Elizabeth's Christocentric orientation, is fundamentally the same as that to which all Christian believers are called: an authentic Christian existence flows into praise of God—praise of the glory of God, praise of the grace of God that is manifested in Christ. In her praise of the glory of God Elizabeth too gathered up her entire life, all the experiences of her adolescence, and her acts of faith

---

[93] To Rev. Chevignard, L244, October 8, 1905, in *Gli Scritti*, p. 380.

[94] According to M. Philipon, Elizabeth discovered her "new name" not before the spring or summer of 1905. He bases this date on the witness of an elderly religious given thirty years after the death of Elizabeth. More recent scholars, however, have discovered, based on a more accurate dating of her letters, that the vocation to be "praise of glory" goes back to the beginning of 1904, therefore preceding her celebrated "O My God, Trinity Whom I Adore." Therefore a necessary correction must be made to M. Philipon's theory according to which Elizabeth, in her "Hymn to the Trinity," did not feel completely liberated from herself, from her impotence to come out of herself, and only with the discovery of her new name was she able to give herself freely. Cf. M. Philipon, *La Dottrina Spirituale di Elisabetta della Trinità* (Brescia, ca. 1945), p. 141.

from her "nights" of the spirit. After her health crisis in April 1906 and in the final months of her life, she understood that she was called to reveal the praise of the glory that radiates from the face of Christ Crucified. The fullness of her vocation, begun here, reached an unimagined profundity of abandonment, from which would blossom an even more profound name: "victim-host of praise."

For this reason, Elizabeth begged Canon Angles to consecrate her "like a little victim-host of praise who wants to glorify Him [God] in heaven and on earth, in suffering, for as long as He desires."[95] In her next letter to him she wrote, "After I wrote you it seemed heaven opened again" ... and now more than ever I realize I am "a prisoner who in the intimacy of his soul sings the love of his Maestro night and day."[96]

In July she asked Canon Angles, as a gift for her birthday, "I want to consecrate myself at Mass like a victim-host of praise to the glory of God. Oh, consecrate me wholly so that I am no longer myself, *but Him*, and the Father, looking at me, might recognize that I am 'conformed to His death' ... and then immerse me in the blood of Christ, so that I am strong by His very own strength."[97]

Recalling the anniversary of her entrance into Carmel, she asked Fr. Vallée to pray that she rise "to Calvary as the bride of the Crucified" and to consecrate her to the Three as a tiny victim-host of praise. A few lines earlier she had written, "Until He glorifies me, I want to be the unceasing praise of His glory."[98]

---

[95] To Canon Angles, L271, May 9, 1906, in *Gli Scritti*, p. 406.

[96] To Canon Angles, L275, early June 1906, in *Gli Scritti*, p. 420.

[97] To Canon Angles, L294, July 8 or 9, 1906, in *Gli Scritti*, pp. 433–434.

[98] To Fr. Vallée, L304, August 2, 1906, in *Gli Scritti*, pp. 449–450.

This thought returned at the beginning of the *Last Retreat* with greater insight. Christ has become "the perfect praise of His Father's glory"[99] in drinking from the bitter chalice of the Passion. "I want to take this chalice, purple with the blood of my Maestro and, in giving thanks, filled with joy, mix my blood with that of the Holy Victim, so that my blood acquires, in a certain sense, an infinite worth and can give splendid praise to the Father."[100] In this union of blood, Christ, likened to the sun, arrives as a "devouring fire" from which none can escape. And so "the blessed transformation of which John of the Cross speaks saying, 'Each seems to be the other and both are nothing but one,' to be 'praise of glory' of the Father,"[101] is brought about. This is possible because at this point the soul has been completely emptied and there is liberation from all that does not belong to pure love and to God's glory.

Of course, the musical chords of the Elizabethan lyre no longer vibrate in exuberant joy. The melodic waves of her evening prayer have something of the pathetic, without being morbid, when they rise in silent majesty to the beloved God, accompanying the "Mass He celebrates together with me," that Mass that is pure sacrifice, immolation of the "little victim-host" on the altar of life.[102]

These are the harmonies of the one from whom everything has been stripped away; the reflections of a bold voyage toward a deeper reality, both natural and supernatural; the final yearning of the entire spiritual existence of Elizabeth of the Trinity.

[99] *Last Retreat*, 1.1, in *Gli Scritti*, p. 636.
[100] Ibid., 7.18, in *Gli Scritti*, p. 645.
[101] Ibid., 7.19, in *Gli Scritti*, p. 646.
[102] To her mother, L309, ca. September 9, 1906, in *Gli Scritti*, p. 456.

From that moment on, the initiative is entirely God's. Her praise, offered as a host that plunges her into the ocean of her Three, drowns her in the secret mystery of God. Identified with the Crucified, the dying Carmelite has "passed wholly into Him, and He in her." Solitude, silence, and oblation constitute the climate in which Elizabeth finds herself beholding the intensity of the Father's work that had pushed her to bear the image of Christ in herself, so that this image might emanate with always-greater clarity.

In the Crucified her desire to make of her soul a heaven that ceaselessly sings the "glory of the Eternal One" and *nothing other than the glory of the Eternal One*," found its ultimate expression.[103] With this praise on her lips and in her heart Elizabeth, having become a living doxology of the greatness of God, ends her earthly pilgrimage in order to accomplish *in aeternum*, thrust into the bosom of the Trinity, the "praise of His glory."

WITH THE VIRGIN MARY

It was Mary, the faithful Virgin, adorer of the Word Incarnate, "the great praise of glory of the Holy Trinity"[104] who accompanied Elizabeth on her interior journey. Elizabeth placed the Mother of Jesus at the summit of the spiritual journey; she was the one in whom Elizabeth's idea of virginal and Carmelite perfection was perfectly and completely realized, both on the part of the salvific action of God and on the part of human cooperation. Mary, "Mother and Queen," is present in her poems and meditations,

---

[103] *Last Retreat*, 7.17, in *Gli Scritti*, p. 645.
[104] *Last Retreat*, 15.40, in *Gli Scritti*, p. 659.

where her fascination with the Marian mysteries as fount of loving inspiration for living the silent riches of Mary's existence can be seen.

> Mother of the Word, tell me your mystery.
> After the incarnation of the Lord,
> as upon the earth you passed
> all buried in adoration.
> In unspeakable peace,
> in mysterious silence,
> you penetrated the Unfathomable
> carrying within you "the gift of God."
> Preserve me always
> in a divine embrace,
> that I might carry within me the imprint
> of this God–All Love.[105]

Here the image of Mary is defined with the nuance of the contemplation of the silent adorer of the mystery of the Incarnation. She must have been very dear to Elizabeth, who spoke of her in her *Retreats* as well. In the last period of her life Elizabeth was glad to speak with the Sorrowful Mother in a spirit of trust and intimacy.

Mary, as the perfect image of praise to the Trinity, is a particularly important image. From reading the subtle songs that Elizabeth reserved for her, it is apparent how Elizabeth's heart vibrated with the immense desire to imitate Mary in her constant commitment to practicing virtue, in her continual effort to live in God's presence within her, in her maintaining interior

---

[105] Poem 88, in *Gli Scritti*, p. 756.

recollection, and above all in her passionate love, which explodes in the Magnificat:

> To love is to imitate Mary
> magnifying the greatness of God
> as when enraptured
> she lifted her song to the Lord [the Magnificat].
> Your core, O faithful Virgin,
> was annihilation,
> because Jesus, eternal Splendor,
> hides in lowliness.
> It is in humility that your soul
> raises the Magnificat.[106]

In the prayer on the tenth day of *Heaven in Faith* Elizabeth enters into a dialogue of admiration with "a creature who was so luminous and pure that she seemed to be light itself.... A creature whose life was so simple and lost in God that it is almost impossible to speak about it." This creature is Mary, the faithful Virgin, she who "kept in her heart all the words of God," the whole mystery of Christ. For this reason she did not withdraw from her silence. "She remained so very little and attentive to God's presence, in the secret of the temple, that she attracted the pleasure of the Holy Trinity." Contemplating Mary in her humble adoration, the Father bends down over this creature and the Spirit of Love intervenes. "The Virgin speaks her fiat: 'Behold the handmaid of the Lord, let it be done unto me according to thy word,'" and the greatest of all mysteries

---

[106] Poem 94, in *Gli Scritti*, p. 764. The last two lines are translated by the author from the French original, *J'ai trouvé Dieu*, vol. II, p. 376.

was then fulfilled. And in the descent of the Word, Mary was forever God's prey."

This behavior of the Virgin seems to Elizabeth to be "a model of interior souls, of those creatures whom God has chosen to live interiorly, at the bottom of the bottomless abyss."

That expression "bottomless abyss" echoes passages of the Flemish mystic Jan Ruusbroec from Ernest Hello's anthology, *Oeuvres choisies*, which Elizabeth read in that period. From the moment of her fiat, Mary lived her humble existence at "the bottom of the soul, a bottom as deep as an abyss." There within, God possessed her like a "prey"—a term that Elizabeth liked to use, but that was not her own. Already before entering Carmel, reading Thérèse of Lisieux's *Story of a Soul* and copying long passages from it, Elizabeth had made her own the Thérèsian image of the divine Eagle that clutches us like prey and, "placing us on His wings, carries us far away, to glorious heights, where the soul and the heart love to lose themselves."[107] Applying this image to Mary, it seems to Elizabeth that all souls must become "prey." "It is so wonderful to belong to Him, to be completely His, His prey, His victim of love!"[108]

Love that gives without limit, that attempts to lose itself in the Other, that searches passionately to exceed the possibilities of its own strength, ends by seeing itself as a prey destined to annihilation by a superabundance of love. "Aimer, aimer tout le temps, vivre d'amour, c'est-à-dire être sa proie! To love, to

---

[107] Letter to Marguerite Gollot, L41, February 18, 1901, *Gli Scritti*, p. 112. (The date is ascertained based on the contents of the letter.)

[108] Letter to Marguerite Gollot, L54, May 16, 1901, *Gli Scritti*, p. 127

love always, to live love, means to be handed over, to be His prey."[109]

These last exclamations, scribbled on a note to a fellow novice, Helene Cantener, who left Carmel after a few months, correspond to Elizabeth's secret desire: to realize in her own life a love that is transformed into complete abandonment to God. This is Mary's behavior, and it ought to be imitated by all Christians. How? It is enough to look to the Virgin. "With what peace, with what recollection Mary approached everything, accomplished everything! Even the most insignificant things were divinized by Mary! In all and for all the Virgin remained in adoration of the gift of God. That did not keep her from giving lavishly of herself in matters of charity." She was able to do so because she immersed herself in the "ineffable vision that she contemplated within herself,"[110] Christ, the divine Word.

In the meditations from day fifteen of Elizabeth's *Last Retreat*, it is easy to see how Mary, adorer of Christ present in her womb, is also at the same time a perfect praise of the Trinity. She is the "pure, immaculate, irreproachable" Virgin, attributes taken from Colossians 1:22 and applied to Mary, not without reference to the "Most Pure" (a title by which Mary was for centuries venerated in Carmel) and "Immaculate" (this was fifty years after the dogmatic proclamation, although the feast of the Immaculate Conception is the Carmelites' most ancient Marian feast). This woman, companion of Christ in the work of salvation, sang the most beautiful praises of the grandeur of God.

---

[109] To Helene Cantener, L125, after June 21, 1902, only in the French edition and cited in *J'ai trouvé Dieu*, vol. Ib, p. 94.
[110] *Heaven in Faith*, 10.1, in *Gli Scritti*, pp. 629–630.

We need to unite ourselves to Mary, Elizabeth repeats, in order to be the perfect praise of the Omnipotent; imitate her as the humble "handmaid of the Lord, the least of his creatures"; and find strength in her martyrdom at the foot of the Cross. "She remained there, standing next to the Cross, strong and heroic." She should be contemplated "so serene in her majesty, conveying both strength and sweetness." Christ Crucified gave her to us like that, as Mother; and we must take her as a model in our suffering.

At this point Elizabeth passes to a personal reflection: now that Jesus "has returned to His Father and He has put me in His place on the cross ... the Virgin is still there to teach me how to suffer as He did, to tell me, to help me understand, those final songs of His [Christ's] soul which no one beside her was able to perceive. When I will have cried my 'consummatum est,' it will be she, *Janua Coeli*, who will introduce me in the eternal tabernacles, whispering the mysterious word: 'Laetatus sum in his quae dicta sunt mihi, in domum Domini ibimus!' "[111] "Janua Coeli," "Heaven's Gate," an invocation of the Litany of Loreto, was often repeated by Elizabeth in her final months, revealing her filial and most tender trust in the intercession of the Mother of God at the hour of her death.

The passage cited above, which uses well-known Marian elements interwoven with intimate personal feelings, could be part of a mystical medieval Marian praise. It is a mysterious conversation with the Sorrowful Mother beneath the Cross, in which

---

[111] *Last Retreat* 15.40. The Dijon Carmelites recited Psalm 122 ("I was glad when they said to me, 'Let us go to the house of the LORD!'" [Ps. 122:1]) three times a day as they processed into choir. (A choir is a room lined with choir stalls situated adjacent to the chapel sanctuary. —Trans.)

Elizabeth would like to feel the final sighs of Christ's soul and undergo the luminous radiance of the Man-God's return to the Father's breast at the end of the human struggle. This conversation enabled her to trust that she would go to the house of the Lord guided by Mary's hand. Hers would also be a return in which eternal joy would triumph over the drama of human weakness, melting away under the maternal hand of the Queen of Heaven. "I cry for joy," she wrote to her sister, Marguerite, "thinking that this creature, all-serene, all-luminous, is my Mother."[112]

In Mary the whole history of human suffering and sadness acquires a new expression. In Elizabeth that same history carried her toward transfiguration in that light that encircles the Mother of God, who stands with her Risen Son. The Marian message of the Dijon Carmelite is therefore a warm invitation to all those who live interiorly in the depths to open themselves to the influence of Mary, she who leads them to be, together with Christ, the image of God, the model of singing eternal praise to God.

---

[112] To her sister, Marguerite, L298, July 16, 1906, in *Gli Scritti*, p. 439.

CHAPTER THREE

A CONTEMPLATIVE WOMAN

MYSTICAL INTUITION

All the saints and spiritual masters teach that the encounter with God "there within," in the "heaven of the soul," is realized in only one way: by rejecting and transcending the entire created world, so fragile and passing, and most of all ourselves and our own works.

"One must separate himself from everything so to possess Him who is All,"[113] wrote Elizabeth to her mother. This was not the only time in her writings that she recalled that unceasing effort needed to bring oneself into the presence of God perceived in the depth of the spirit, an effort that requires a continuous battle fought one step at a time.

This is the way of Carmel, where the novice and the young professed are educated to mortification, to overcoming self, to living "separated, stripped of everything" except God.

Teresa of Ávila and John of the Cross told her that there are no "wide and easy streets to be traveled, but only thorny

[113] To her mother, L170, ca. August 13, 1903, in *Gli Scritti*, p. 261.

paths" that, winding "through brambles," bring one to union with God.

Elizabeth did not hide from herself that this meant a daily death; otherwise, "we can be hidden in God in certain hours of the day, but we cannot *live* habitually in the Divine Being, because feelings, personal interests, and all the rest will carry us away."[114]

These autobiographical words are inserted into the *Last Retreat*, and it is easy to recognize traces of John of the Cross's doctrine as explained in his *Spiritual Canticle*.

Beginning in 1902, after receiving the fourth volume of the *Complete Works* of John of the Cross, including both the *Spiritual Canticle* and *Living Flame of Love*, Elizabeth made good use of these works quite often.[115] It became "the entire nourishment of her soul."[116]

With awe she immersed herself in those pages that address the transformation *by love*, copying and marking passages that particularly struck her because they corresponded perfectly to her spirit and her experience.

Finding "little gems" that related to the letters of St. Paul and the Gospel of St. John, the mystical doctor of Carmel [St. John of the Cross] acquired great significance for Elizabeth's spiritual

---

[114] *Last Retreat*, 6.16, in *Gli Scritti*, p. 644.

[115] M. D. Poinsenet, *Questa Presenza di Dio in te* (Milano: Ancora, 1971), p. 208. The author remembers that in that book, seventeen pages of *Living Flame of Love* were found that Elizabeth had annotated with certain symbols, which she must have used to remember the dominant thought that had struck her and echoes of which can be found in her later letters. Elizabeth had the edition that was edited by the Carmelites of Paris, vol. IV (Paris, 1892).

[116] To M. Antonietta de Bobet, L241, August 17, 1905, in *Gli Scritti*, p. 374.

progress. She even called him "my blessed Father," as a sign of her preference for his mystical doctrine summarized in the themes of: the search for God, spousal love (along the lines of the Song of Songs), prayer, union lived with diligence in "the deepest center of the self" where God is present, solitude, and silence.[117]

Especially in her final months, Elizabeth gave hints of her interior journey, traveled under the guidance of the Carmelite father toward the heights of mystical love.

"St. John of the Cross says that 'it is in the very essence of the soul, where neither demons nor the world can penetrate, that God gives Himself to her.'[118] Immersed in this divine presence it results that all the soul's movements are divine, because they are worked by God, who is the center of the soul." But in order to arrive "at the deepest center," of which John of the Cross speaks, it is necessary to love God with "all one's strength" and to enjoy Him entirely, to meet Him in pure heaven, full of divine presence. "Since it is love that unites, the more intense the love is, the more deeply one enters into God and is centered in Him." When [the soul] "possesses even one degree of love, it is already in its center; but when this love will have reached its perfection, the soul will be penetrated in its '*deepest* center.' It is there that it will be transformed to the point of becoming very much like God."[119] Here Elizabeth revealed that life had become one great act of love.

In addition to St. John of the Cross, who enlightened her time of solitude in the infirmary, Elizabeth discovered Jan Ruusbroec

[117] To her sister, Marguerite, L239, August 17, 1905, in *Gli Scritti*, p. 370. In reference to John of the Cross, *Living Flame of Love*, B, 1, 12–13.

[118] *Living Flame of Love*, B, 1.9.

[119] *Heaven in Faith*, 2.1, in *Gli Scritti*, p. 611.

through Ernest Hello's famous anthology.[120] In fact, in the pages of her two *Retreats* are found passages from Ruusbroec copied almost word for word. Elizabeth often adopts the Flemish mystic's expressions to synthesize or better express her own thought.

It is important to remember that Elizabeth also frequently drew from Angela of Foligno's *Libro*.[121]

During the long hours of suffering, she consoled herself by studying others' mystical experiences. As a matter of fact, she was happy to have inherited them, making use of them as a contemplative in need of spiritual nourishment. In them can be discovered common threads that recall her own experience, her ability to make them her own in support of her own message, as we will have opportunity to examine and highlight.

The Abyss of Love

Every contemplative life is founded upon the total self-donation to God in order to love Him above every other thing, with the hope of feeling oneself loved by Him with a profound and transforming love.

Elizabeth Catez was one of these contemplatives.

In words borrowed from John of the Cross, she wanted to make her life a lively and enthusiastic effort to arrive at the highest expressions of love for God.

---

[120] *Ruusbroec l'admirable, Oeuvres choisies*, trans. Ernest Hello (Paris: Perrin, 1902).

[121] *Le livre des visions et instructions de la bienheureuse Angèle de Foligno*, trans. Ernest Hello (1893). The English translation of St. Angela of Foligno's work is entitled simply *Book*. — Trans.

St. John of the Cross, the great doctor of love ... says that "God likes nothing other than love. We cannot give Him anything, nor can we satisfy His only desire, which is that of bringing about the dignity of our souls. The one thing that is pleasing to Him is that the soul grows; but nothing can raise it like becoming, in a certain way, equal to God. That is why He demands from the soul the tribute of its love: the characteristic of love is to make the lover equal to the beloved. The exercise of loving makes the soul equal to the beloved Christ. Love establishes the unity."[122]

It was this *unity of love* that Elizabeth nurtured in her personal aspirations, and nothing could disturb the desires of her heart. Stripped of every earthly attachment, she abandoned herself to Christ, her beloved Spouse, like "'the turtledove that finds on the grassy shores her long-desired companion.' Yes, 'I found Him whom my soul loves,' that One Thing Necessary whom no one can take from me."[123] She said this knowing well that from all eternity God had "loved her to excess."[124]

---

[122] To Mother Jeanne of the Blessed Sacrament, prioress of the Dominican Sisters, nurses of the poor, L274, June 3, 1906, in *Gli Scritti*, p. 408.

[123] To Canon Angles, September 1902, in *Gli Scritti*, p. 216. The reference is to John of the Cross's *Spiritual Canticle* B, 34. The author does not give the number of the letter. In the English translation, *Complete Works: Letters from Carmel*, vol. II (Washington, DC: ICS Publications, 1995), pp. 59–60, letter 131 is addressed to Canon Angles and contains this text. The date ascribed in the English translation, however, is August 2, 1902. — Trans.

[124] Cf. Poem 122, October 9, 1906, in *Gli Scritti*, p. 784.

Propter nimiam charitatem: these words from Ephesians 2:4 guided Elizabeth above all in this last phase; therefore, she directed her gaze to that "superabundance" that at a certain point broke into her existence. She felt overcome by something that she could not totally grasp, but that she would have liked to proclaim with exultation, gratitude, and admiration. "There is a word of St. Paul that is like a summary of my life and that could be written on each moment of it: 'propter nimiam charitatem.' Yes, this torrent of grace shows that 'He has loved me 'excessively' "[125]—excessively, that is, for a creature who for "the past five years" had considered herself "a prisoner of His love." Radiant with happiness, Elizabeth abandoned herself to the experience of being "loved to excess."[126]

In this experience there is a particular mystical intuition, prepared for through her efforts to understand better "the science of charity of which St. Paul speaks and of which my heart would like to plumb the depths."[127]

Her attraction to the biblical concept of "excess" is beyond all understanding. Elizabeth intuits that there is a bottomless abyss in which she can lose herself, a mysterious abyss that in Elizabeth's understanding transforms itself into the invisible and immoveable Reality from which all things proceed.

The loss of self in the abyss of love resonated with her reading of Ruusbroec, "L'amour est un abîme, et le fond d'abîme n'existe pas."[128] "I read magnificent things," she wrote to her sister, referring to the doctrine of the Flemish mystic. "He constantly speaks

---

[125] To her mother, L280, June 12, 1906, in *Gli Scritti*, p. 446.

[126] To Sr. Marie-Philippe, L303, August 2, 1906, in *Gli Scritti*, p. 446.

[127] To Canon Angles, L219, January 1905, in *Gli Scritti*, p. 332.

[128] " Love is an abyss, and there is no bottom to the abyss."

of that interior 'abyss' into which we must throw ourselves and in which we lose ourselves, the abyss of love that we possess within ourselves and in which beatitude awaits us if we are faithful in entering into it."[129]

From the writings of Ruusbroec she had picked up that "the abyss of God calls the elect to a unity of love.... United to the spirit of God ... we possess beatitude with Him and in Him."[130]

Through her readings of Ruusbroec, this image of the abyss — previously used by Elizabeth more or less spontaneously — acquired for her a new and particular luminosity because it was tightly bound to the "excess" of the love of God, being a symbol of the absolute immeasurability of love's greatness.

In one of her final poems, under St. Angela of Foligno's influence, she even speaks of the "double abyss" — the abyss of God's immensity and the abyss of man's nothingness[131] — and invites all to throw themselves into that abyss so as to consummate their love in the divine union, which will be "the most sublime praise" that can be raised to the Almighty Lord.[132]

The abyss of the divine immensity cannot be reached except through the action of grace. But the abyss of one's own nothingness is defeated through an arduous battle against one's self,

---

[129] To her sister, Marguerite, L292, early July 1906, in *Gli Scritti*, p. 435.

[130] *Ruusbroec*, pp. 52–53.

[131] *The Greatness of Our Vocation*, where she cites the *Book* probably from memory: "le double abîme, où l'Immensité divine est en tête-à-tête avec néant de l'homme." *J'ai trouvé Dieu*, vol. Ia, 19, p. 136. "Il doppio abisso, O l'Immensita divina e in una faccia-a-faccia con il niente dell'uomo." (The double abyss, O Divine Immensity, is in a face-to-face encounter with man's nothingness.)

[132] Poem 118, in *Gli Scritti*, p. 783.

because it is "there below that we will find the strength to die to ourselves ... and we will be changed in love."[133]

There is a whole plan of descent in self-denial that must be carried out: decrease each day so that Christ may increase.

Elizabeth felt she must stay "very small 'at the bottom of my poverty.' I see 'my nothingness, my misery, my impotence. I recognize that I am incapable of progress or of perseverance. I behold the multitude of my negligences, of my defects; I look at my neediness. I prostrate myself in my misery and openly recognize it, I expose it to the mercy" of my Maestro. "Quotidie morior"[134] (1 Cor. 15:31).

Christ is the model of this descent with His word of self-denial, doing only what the Father wills. Having arrived at the bottom of the abyss—which is the work of a lifetime—and when all "our vestiges" (our "self," which always tends to affirm itself) are lost, God is free to intervene as a "devouring fire." The soul can "throw herself into the furnace of burning love" in this abyss, and there will be no other preoccupation in her but that of "allowing herself to burn" in the flames of the Holy Spirit. Then "'sweetly lost in God'... 'love fills her so much, absorbs her and protects her' so well, that 'she finds the secret of growing in love everywhere.'"[135]

Up to this point Elizabeth's doctrine of surrender has consisted in self-denial and in throwing oneself into the abyss of nothing, building upon the teachings of John of the Cross and Ruusbroec. While her doctrine addresses God's intervention through both

[133] *Heaven in Faith*, 1.2, in *Gli Scritti*, p. 610.
[134] Ibid., 3.2, in *Gli Scritti*, p. 613.
[135] Ibid., 4.2, in *Gli Scritti*, pp. 615–616.

communications and passive experiences, it does not go beyond the realm of faith. "So we know and believe the love God has for us" (1 John 4:16).

Nevertheless there is an original insight in Elizabeth's thought.

It is not enough to believe in God's great love based on the theological knowledge of revelation, of the divine action in relationship to each person's history.

It is necessary to believe in the excess of this love, to have the faith that is founded on the fact that God is love, that the inner life of God is a relationship of intimate love in which each human person is called to share as an adopted son and as an icon of God Himself. This faith "is the means by which we can give God love in return for love"—she is obviously thinking of a correspondence of love—"a faith, that is, that is not an intellectual act, but wisdom, right judgment, experiential knowledge, which consents to 'penetrate into,' to arrive all the way at 'the heart of the Father' ... and our whole soul is astounded."[136]

Such a faith, one that "knows it must believe in 'an excessive love,'" acquires a remarkable ability to free the soul from "personal tastes and feelings"; in fact, "little does it matter whether it feels God or not, little does it matter if He gives joy or suffering, the soul believes in His love. The more she is tested, the more her faith grows, because she knows to go beyond the obstacles

---

[136] Ibid., 6.1, in *Gli Scritti*, p. 618. Elizabeth cites from memory lines from a letter she received from Fr. Vallée: "Nous, nous avons connu l'amour que Dieu a pour nous *et nous y avons cru*. ... Croire que nous sommes aimés ainsi, c'est le grand acte de notre foi, c'est le moyen de rendre à notre Dieu crucifié amour pour amour ... et tout notre coeur tressaillant enfin sous la vie qui déborde et pour laquelle il est fait." Cf. *J'ai trouvé Dieu*, vol. Ia, 11b, p. 109.

and rest in the bosom of Infinite Love, who can do nothing but works of love."[137] This love tends to increase, to grow more absolute, but does not disengage from the faith that raises its voice with groans and hope toward God-Charity. "It seems to me that this must be the behavior of a praise of glory," continues Elizabeth in the *Last Retreat*, "to be 'unwavering in his faith' in this 'excessive love,' as if he had seen the Invisible."[138]

A TRINITARIAN MYSTICAL LIFE

At this point one could ask if this Carmelite of Dijon was a mystic.

If "mystic" means extraordinary experiences, visions, revelations, locutions, and other supernatural phenomena, it would be difficult to call Elizabeth a mystic. If instead a broader concept of what it means to be a mystic is accepted, including particular illuminations and graces that consent to a lived understanding that goes beyond the usual spiritual path, then without a doubt Elizabeth Catez was a mystic.

In any case, it is preferable to describe her interior life as a *mystical life*, using terms of mystical experience in reference to her with a certain prudence.

The mystical *life* is distinguished from the mystical *experience* because it does not require an explicit awareness of direct intervention from God in one's life.

---

[137] *Heaven on Earth*, 6.2, in *Gli Scritti*, p. 619.
[138] *Last Retreat*, 4.10, in *Gli Scritti*, p. 640.

It places the Christian mysteries at the center of faith, hope, and love; it grows in openness to the movements of the Holy Spirit; it requires an atmosphere of silence and solitude; and it seeks to arrive at "rest" in God, at a peace and a profound serenity in the presence of the Lord.

All of this was found in Elizabeth of Dijon. She lived it in a simplified manner even before she became a Carmelite.

In fact, one notes her uncommon ability to discern God's presence in nature and to live this presence in her search for a world beyond this one.

◈

Elizabeth was a contemplative by nature.

Her gaze fixed upon the sea, the mountains, and the horizon, questioning them about that "excess of Love" that goes beyond the visible reality and whose effects she intuited.

Hers was the intuition of an artistically gifted, although not refined, soul; a soul capable of perceiving melodies and sounds as revelations of Love that told her she was loved in return by the highest Beauty.

It was also the intuition of a soul in love, that turned her attention toward a Magnificence that can be neither apprehended nor described, knowing that she could believe that it exists as Love beyond all visible reality. Elizabeth shivered with joy thinking of the Infinite who stooped down over her and bestowed on her meager life unhoped-for intimacy in a religious experience of love.

Upon entering at Carmel, Elizabeth began to live like a little bride preparing for her wedding to Jesus (on the day of her Profession). If previously Elizabeth had favored the spousal dimension of her spiritual journey—a bit like the medieval women mystics—from that day she considered herself truly "Jesus' bride," forever united to Him by an indissoluble bond.

One letter witnesses: "I am finally all His and He is all mine; I have nothing but Him, He is my All! And now I have but one desire, to love Him, *to love Him in every moment*, to exalt His honor and shape His happiness, like a true bride [allusion to the *Vespers* of St. Teresa of Ávila], to make Him happy by preparing Him a dwelling and a refuge in my soul, where by the power of love I can help Him forget all the injustices and evils of the earth."[139] And in return the Groom will not deny the little Carmelite of Dijon His firm presence in the depth of her soul.

"Passing the day beside the Groom" filled the mystical life of Elizabeth not with sweet feelings, but with a new joy that enriched her solitude and the poverty of her life. "So," said Elizabeth, "all the rest disappears and I lose myself in Him like a drop of water in the ocean, in calm and infinite serenity, the peace of the good God, of whom St. Paul speaks when he says this 'surpasses every feeling.'"[140]

The image of the ocean, so dear to Elizabeth, and repeatedly used with deep echoes of St. Thérèse's writings, led to the image of the abyss. A drop of water thrown into the immensity of the ocean waters disappears in the vast abyss of God without the slightest sound. And the Carmelite felt an interior opening within, "a profound silence which I never want to abandon."[141]

Elizabeth did not tire of searching for the abyss of God in the depth of her soul and casting herself in. As was seen, this echoed Ruusbroec.

---

[139] To Mrs. Angles, L156, February 15, 1903, in *Gli Scritti*, p. 239.
[140] To Canon Angles, L190, January 4, 1904, in *Gli Scritti*, p. 286.
[141] Ibid.

Here the mystical life, identified with the spousal life and a life of love, is lived out in the soul, where solitude, silence, and absolute emptiness reign. It is therefore necessary to lose oneself, bury oneself in this abyss, that is, to welcome within oneself the initiatives of divine love and abandon oneself more fully to the interior movements.

This is why the monastic from Dijon repeatedly remarked about her need to retire in interior silence.

The Rule of Carmel teaches: "Your strength will be to stay in silence." Elizabeth absorbed this. A few months before dying, she would find it necessary to remember that in order to "maintain her strength for the Lord," she must "unify her whole being through interior silence."[142]

Looking at her own life, she could witness to the great help her faithful practice of living in silence was to her exercise of love and to being "a perfect praise of glory" who sings the "*canticum magnum*."[143]

In Elizabeth's doctrine there is no strict distinction between interior and exterior silence. One presupposes the other. Exterior silence serves interior silence because it embraces a way of asceticism, of purification, of renunciations, of death, leading up to the experience of that terrible way of the "nights of St. John." Silence is of maximum importance particularly in relationship to *recollection*: it is the necessary atmosphere for seeking the divine presence in the soul, "to live alone with God alone."

In her efforts to find the mysterious transcendent world of silence, Elizabeth was firmly tied to the mystical science of John of the Cross.

[142] *Last Retreat*, 2.3, in *Gli Scritti*, p. 636.
[143] Ibid., p. 637.

It is easy to pick out in her writings the passages from the *Spiritual Canticle* and the *Living Flame of Love* (copied by her or cited from memory) which guided her thought and confirmed her experience.

The same can be said regarding *exterior solitude*.

In Carmel it was no longer the mountains and the sea surrounding her with their irresistible enticement of solitude. Now this allurement was found in the little "paradise" of her cell, where she passed many hours of her day, and where she encountered the great Solitary. In the "little shrine" of her cell, Christ her Groom helped her understand that in order to ascend to God's realm—which is perfection—one must become "a great Solitary."

God is completely Other, and "He lives in an eternal, immense solitude, from which He never departs, despite His interest in the needs of His creatures. In fact, He never leaves Himself; and this solitude is nothing other than His divinity." Consequently, one must not "leave interior silence"—that is, the separation from, or stripping away of, the world—since "if my desires, my fears, my joys or my pains, if all the motions borne of these 'four passions' are not perfectly ordered to God, I will not be a solitary; there will be noise in me."[144]

In this richness of mystical life is undoubtedly expressed, by flashes or allusions, the light of supernatural grace passively accepted by Elizabeth.

Beyond these fleeting hints we have her marvelous prayer, the "Hymn to the Trinity," in which the creative power of the Holy Spirit that descended into Elizabeth's heart with particular illuminations cannot be denied. Also her immersion in the

---

[144] *Last Retreat*, 10.26.

mystery of God, echoed in her *Personal Notes*, in some letters and poems, and especially in the last two *Retreats*, demands a presumption of some communication from above.

Of course, the desire to receive divine communications was alive in her, and this brought about a general integration of her interior life.

Although not everything can be interpreted as an actual intervention of God, it cannot be denied that the way in which Elizabeth explained certain concepts and themes of interior experience and the capacity to enter into the mysticism of St. Paul and St. John of the Cross are shocking in such a young monastic who had an insufficient education and theological-spiritual formation.

Her ease in applying nuances to herself beyond the objective facts evokes the presence of interior illuminations welcomed in her soul like mysterious touches of grace, expressed like sketched notes of a symphony, and lived in an interpersonal dimension.

Proper weight must be given to the terms she used to describe, for example, the indwelling of the Trinity in her soul. She spoke of a feeling, a possessing, even of a seeing [of Him]. Having reached the end of her earthly journey, she confided to Mother Germana of Jesus: "The Holy Trinity let me *feel* His presence in my soul; it seemed to me to *see* the three divine Persons holding council in me."[145]

The same desire to want to be lost, buried in the bosom of the Trinity presupposes, in a certain sense, an experiential fact.

The witnesses for the process of her beatification affirmed in agreement that she was "profoundly penetrated by the Trinity present in her soul, so as even to feel it physically. In one

---

[145] *Summarium*, p. 193.

encounter, in fact, she says: 'I think He is here,' accompanying her words with a gesture of one holding something to his heart."[146]

Finally, her experiences of profound pain that joined her to Christ's Passion must not be forgotten. Her ascent to Calvary during the "dark nights"—when she had to endure being stripped bare, the emptiness, the pain, God's silence, the destruction that immersed her in the shadows of the spirit—is related to experiences that can be interpreted as direct interventions of God in the soul.

Elizabeth knew the passive purification through which all mystics have passed.

She lived in pain for a long time, but she knew how to transform it into love, caressing it with a contemplative glance, as a yoking to the beloved Christ who died on the Cross.

APOSTOLIC CONTEMPLATIVE LIFE

"To pray and to love can be a beautiful occupation, but how can it be reconciled with the gospel command that puts active dedication to one's neighbor as the necessary reply? All the more so since in Christianity we adore a God made man who explicitly declared that He considers done (or not done) to Him that which is done (or not done) to the least of His brothers."[147]

This question might be asked of all consecrated contemplatives.

---

[146] Ibid., p. 345.
[147] Cf. A. Sicari, *Elisabetta della Trinità: Un'esistenza teologica* (Rome, 1984), p. 135.

It is not easy to comprehend an existence completely dedicated to the praise of God, lacking commitments or activities directed at helping others.

Christians, and sometimes even priests, do not doubt the importance of making plenty of time for prayer. At the same time, however, they are unable to find the link between the primacy (or even exclusivity) of the work of prayer and the urgent needs, of all sorts, of the modern world.

It is true, from prayer offered for every possible situation streams the grace of divine intervention, but there fails to be an openness to departure from the world in order to be solely dedicated to prayer, to fulfill, like Elizabeth Catez, a vocation of "praise of glory to God" within the confines of a monastery.

❧

In her choice of Carmel, Elizabeth had faced this problem during turbulent times of anticlericalism and the suppression of many convents. The separation of church and state was proclaimed only five years after she entered Carmel. The monastics were not unaware of the danger that one day the state might suppress their monastery. They had already looked at the possibility of finding refuge in Switzerland and then in Belgium. Nevertheless, in this heated and antireligious climate, the young novices were formed according to the monastic tradition of Carmel, with its absolute primacy of prayer. Not only that: everyone hoped in the power of prayer to avert the threats, to bring peace and Christian life to all of France.

At the Dijon Carmel, the centuries-old Carmelite tradition, following in the footsteps of St. Teresa of Ávila, taught that this very contemplative life ought to be considered ecclesiastical activity.

There is no either-or between contemplation and activity. The Church cannot do without the weapons of prayer that sustain her in spiritual battle. And those entirely dedicated to the contemplative life would not be living their vocation if they did not make the needs of the Church their own, overcoming every individualism and offering prayers and sacrifices for the life of the Mystical Body of Christ.

Elizabeth grew in the conviction that "a Carmelite must be apostolic: all her prayers and all her sacrifices are inclined toward this."[148] She would express this same thought a year later: "Our holy mother Teresa wants all her daughters to be apostolic." For a Carmelite this means participating in Christ's salvific work with a constant commitment to pray for everyone. "Let us also give [Christ] souls."[149] And more precisely: "As a true daughter of St. Teresa, I desire to be an apostle so as to give every glory to Him whom I love. Like my holy Mother I think He left me here on earth to have zeal for His honor like a true bride."[150]

These words were written after her near death in the spring of 1906, but her desire to have zeal for God's glory preceded that episode. Elizabeth expressed her desire as early as February 1903, a month after her Profession, when she was full of happiness at being Christ's bride and passionately desired to love the divine Groom and "to have zeal for His honor."[151]

In her poem "Love," written on occasion of the feast of St. Martha, she develops the idea of what it means to love from the

---

[148] To Germana de Gemeaux, L136, September 14, 1902, in *Gli Scritti*, pp. 212–213.

[149] To Germana de Gemeaux (179), September 20, 1903, in *Gli Scritti*, p. 274.

[150] To Mdme. Hallo, L276, June 7, 1906, in *Gli Scritti*, p. 413.

[151] To Mdme. Angles, L156, February 15, 1903, in *Gli Scritti*, p. 239.

point of view of a Carmelite monastic; in one of the stanzas she highlights their apostolate:

> To love is to be apostles,
> to have zeal for the living God's honor,
> precious ancient inheritance
> left to us by the prophet (Elijah)
> collected by St. Teresa
> and conveyed to her daughters.

Elizabeth makes this her mission, inheriting it in order to interpret it in the light of God's love. The same ideal revealed itself in St. Thérèse of Lisieux's acknowledgment of her desire to be the heart of the Church. An echo of the Thérèsian desire in Elizabeth cannot be excluded when she writes:

> Carmel has become the furnace,
> the hearth of divine Love.

The expression "hearth of love," which returns to Elizabeth's pen especially in her final months, assumes the same meaning as the heart as the most intimate center. Therefore she uses it to affirm with joy:

> Our saints understood this well....
> How they inflamed souls!
> In them, everything gave Jesus Christ,
> radiating His living flames.

An invitation follows: "Let us be true apostles.... With our generosity let us help Holy [Mother] Church."[152]

---

[152] Poem 94, in *Gli Scritti*, pp. 764–765 (author's corrected translation).

ECCLESIASTICAL LIFE

The above poetic composition shows not only that Elizabeth was following the way of the great contemplative-apostolic tradition of Carmel, but also that she let transpire thoughts of the events of the Church of that time, especially in France.

Elizabeth suffers from the sad events of her diocese. On January 25, 1904, she wrote to the seminarian André Chevignard, "My soul loves to unite itself to yours in a shared prayer for the Church and the diocese."[153]

In the diocese there was discussion about how the bishop, Monsignor Le Nordez—well known to the Carmelites—should behave. In 1902, for Elizabeth's reception of the habit, he celebrated with all possible solemnity in the monastery chapel. Only sixteen months later, the chapel was closed to visitors by the state's decree. The monastery remained, but without authorization; [it was] in a certain sense protected by the bishop, but for how long?

The Carmelites, having found a safe haven in Noiseux, Belgium, began to prepare for their departure. In light of the anticipated suppression, some of their furniture was sent ahead. Monsignor Le Nordez was caught in a position of conflict with Rome. He was imprudent and ambitious, and a Republican. There was really very little hope for him. He was accused of favoring the French masons, and there were even rumors, which were false, that he was himself a freemason.

This fact stirred up the local press. Most of the clergy did not know how to respond.

---

[153] To A. Chevignard, L191, January 25, 1904, in *Gli Scritti*, p. 329.

The division between those faithful to Rome and those faithful to the bishop was inevitable. In February, a few days after [Elizabeth had written] the above-mentioned letter [to André Chevignard], the seminarians refused to receive Holy Orders at the hands of Monsignor Le Nordez, who had excluded some of them. By common agreement they rebelled; they left the seminary. The threat of being immediately enrolled in the military, however, made them reconsider and return to the seminary.

Following this incident, the parents of the children scheduled to be confirmed by Bishop Le Nordez refused to bring their children to the cathedral.

In the diocese of Dijon, the tensions continued to grow. Hoping to arrive at a peaceful solution, the priests and faithful of the diocese appealed to Rome. Pius X did not delay in responding with the deposition of Bishop Le Nordez on September 4, 1904.

The appeal to Rome, incorrectly interpreted by the French government, was one of the reasons for the suspension of diplomatic relations between France and the Holy See.

Through her visits in the parlor and news related at recreation by her fellow sisters, Elizabeth was aware of the painful situation in the diocese.

This same seminarian, André Chevignard, her sister Marguerite's brother-in-law, was among the rebel seminarians. Undoubtedly her mother and relatives recounted the particulars of the dramatic days of the seminarians' opposition.

Perhaps Elizabeth had intuited the crisis in Chevignard's soul. In fact, through a careful reading of letter 191, one notes Elizabeth's concern with saving the future priest from the danger of falling: "There are two words that for me summarize holiness and our whole apostolate: union and love." A little before that, she exhorted: "Let us make ourselves holy for souls, since we are all members of one body; in the measure that we abundantly possess divine life, we can communicate [and spread] it to the great Body, the Church." And with the promise "to pray much" for him, "so that on the day of his subdeaconate" — that coming February — "the good God finds your soul as He wants it."[154]

On account of the rebellion, André Chevignard had to wait almost a year.

He was ordained subdeacon on January 6, 1905. Elizabeth received this news with inward joy:

> I unite myself to your emotion and to the profound joy of your soul now as you await ordination, and I ask you to unite me to you in this outpouring of grace; every morning I recite Terce for you so that the Spirit of love and light "descends" into you to produce in you all His creations [allusion to Luke 1:35]. If you would like, we can unite ourselves in one single prayer, reciting the divine office during Terce, to which I have a particular devotion. We will breathe love; we will attract love to our souls and onto the whole Church.[155]

In the first months of 1905, Elizabeth accompanied André Chevignard's preparation for the priesthood with her prayer. In her contemplative soul, she tried to live these important moments together with him, "predestined" by God, chosen to be His priest. "I am convinced that in His action of love, the Father bends over your soul, He molds it with His hand and with His delicate touch, so that ... you will continue to grow

---

[154] Ibid.
[155] To A. Chevignard, L214, November 29, 1904, in *Gli Scritti*, p. 323.

until that day when the Church will tell you: 'You are a priest forever.'"[156]

André Chevignard would be ordained on June 29, 1905, in the cathedral of Dijon by the vicar-general, Monsignor Maillet. The newly ordained priest celebrated Mass in the chapel of Carmel on Friday, June 30, the feast of the Sacred Heart (according to the calendar in use).

It was a day of indescribable happiness in which Elizabeth proposed to accompany him always with her prayer.

She lived in the certainty that God communicated "His divine life in order to transform us into divinized creatures that reflect Him everywhere. What power the apostle who remains forever united to the Wellspring of living water exercises on souls; then he can ... pour out the life of grace all around without running out, because he communicates with the Infinite!" These are words written to another priest, but she would not have expressed herself differently to André Chevignard. "You will be another Christ working for the glory of the Father."

As a contemplative she had the same vocation as a priest, yet on a different plane. "From the bottom of my solitude of Carmel, I want to be an apostle with you. I want to work for the glory of God, and for this I must be completely filled with Him. Thus, I will be omnipotent: a look, a desire becomes an irresistible prayer that can obtain everything, because in a certain way it is God Himself that we offer to God." She could not throw herself into an external apostolate, like the priest who brings the Lord to souls, but "I will remain silent and adoring next to the Maestro, like the Magdalen, begging Him to make

[156] To Rev. Chevignard, L231, early June 1905, in *Gli Scritti*, p. 350–351.

His Word fruitful in souls. 'Apostle' and 'Carmelite' are the same thing."[157]

⚜

Sometimes in comparing Thérèse of Lisieux and Elizabeth of Dijon, the lively sense of the Church is highlighted in the first and seen as missing from the second. But an attentive reading of the writings of the young Carmelite from Dijon will change such a judgment.

Here the ecclesiastical aspect, fully interior, fully centered on God's presence in the soul, as a fecund wellspring of the Church has been highlighted.

To this must be added her desire to live with the Church and her desire to take part in a vital way in the pastoral initiatives of the diocese, which was already manifested in the young Elizabeth during the great mission of 1899.

Her *Diary* allows us to reconstruct her enthusiastic participation. On February 2, in fact, having previously read in the *Semaine religieuse de Dijon* an announcement of the mission, she noted, "We will have an important mission at the end of Lent. I pray already for its success. How I would like to bring souls to my Jesus!"[158] And on February 10, "I take upon myself the world's sins. See no one but me; strike no one but me. I am Your victim, just as I am Your bride, the confidante of Your heart."[159]

After "three marvelous days" she once again declared her intention of offering herself to Jesus with "thoughts," with her sacrifices. "I want to love Him on behalf of all those who do not

---

[157] To Rev. Beaubis, L124, June 22, 1904, in *Gli Scritti*, pp. 305–306.
[158] *Diario*, February 2, 1899, in *Gli Scritti*, p. 519.
[159] Ibid., February 10, 1899, in *Gli Scritti*, p. 521.

love Him; I want to bring back to Him all those souls that He has so loved."

In particular, she thinks of her "landlord, a man with a golden heart and of immense generosity," seventy-three-year-old Henri Chapuis, sadly fallen away from the Faith. "I offered many Communions for this soul, and I count on the mission to fulfill my dream," that is, to see him return to the Faith. "What a joy to have played a small part in this conversion! My God, this would be a great joy! What wouldn't I do for this? Increase my sufferings, good Maestro. I offer my life for the salvation of this soul!"[160]

During the mission Elizabeth's passion for souls matured.

A familiar theme, this, which returned with fiery accents. "I have great thirst to suffer.... I am greedy for sacrifices.... During this mission I feel my flame double. My heart burns with the desire to convert souls."[161] "Souls! May I conquer many!"[162]

Obviously, these are in response to the mission preaching. They evidence the surreal style of the 1800s, the pressure exerted on the human psyche intended to awaken religious enthusiasm.

But this does not preclude a sincere concern for the salvation of souls in Elizabeth and an expectation that the reign of Christ would immediately reestablish peace between the Church and the state.

At Carmel nothing changes this ecclesial attitude of Elizabeth.

At the end of the novitiate, she came to understand better the condition of the Church. She was struck by Pius X's encyclical [*E supremi*] in which he spoke of *instaurare omnia in Christo* [to restore all things in Christ], promulgated on October 4, 1903.

---

[160] Ibid., February 12, 1899, in *Gli Scritti*, p. 521–522.
[161] Ibid., March 7, 1899, in *Gli Scritti*, p. 531.
[162] Ibid., March 9, 1899, in *Gli Scritti*, p. 533.

Elizabeth offered the pope's thought to Mother Germana like "a mystical flower," probably made on the occasion of her much-desired reelection as prioress.

> Mother, remember? In his stupendous encyclical,
> the pope expressed a desire.
> My heart plucked it,
> like a mystical flower
> and here I would like to offer it to you.
> Yes, I dreamed that truly it would be realized in me
> so divine the vow of our sweet Shepherd,
> making His great plan mine too:
> "All to be restored in You,
> my Christ and my Savior."[163]

Availing herself of Pius X's call[164] and connecting it to the "excessive love" of St. Paul, Elizabeth enlarged her glance to her France, increasingly distant from the Faith: "We offer 'the blood of the Just One' to restore France [restaurons aussi le royaume de France]." The blood of Christ 'is our redemption to obtain peace and liberty." God Himself "will pronounce the supreme word of pardon." And she adds that she wants to repeat, in her final hour, the words of Christ:

[163] Poem 89, June 15, 1904, in *Gli Scritti*, pp. 752–754.
[164] Elizabeth had copies of the French translation of the encyclical in the magazine *Semaine religieuse de Dijon*. "Nous declarons que notre but unique dans l'exercice du Suprême Pontificat est de *tout restaurer dans le Christ* afin que *le Christ soit tout en tous....* C'est pourquoi si l'on nous demande une devise (translated by the author with "program" and by the translator with "call," while Elizabeth in the original French used the same word, "device"). *Restaurer toutes les choses dans le Christ*, no. 18, p. 645, cf. *J'ai trouvé Dieu*, vol. II, 3, p. 368.

Father, I made You known, loved;
Your work completed, to You, O God, I return.[165]

In a letter to Canon Angles, Elizabeth recalled the fundamental value of the pope's encyclical for the spiritual apostolate of the Carmelite.

The responsibility is great; the field to plow is arid.

To be "a mediator with Christ" in calamitous times is a responsibility that generated fear in Elizabeth, who knew well her own limits. Her health was in decline; her strength was diminishing day by day. Would she be able to meet the high standards of her intentions during the painful twilight of her illness? And yet, she wanted to offer her sufferings for the Church until the end; and so she did.

THE APOSTOLIC FRUITFULNESS
OF CONTEMPLATIVE PRAYER

These passages from Elizabeth evidence her constant longing to give that which she had received to souls in need of instruction and spiritual help for their conversion.

The Dijon Carmelite repeated that she found herself near the divine wellspring, and, drinking the divine waters, she approached the mysterious riches of Christ's grace to share it with the Church, His priests, her friends, and her acquaintances.

According to her logic, the ability to give or communicate to others depends on the measure one has received, and here

---

[165] Poem 89, June 15, 1904, in *Gli Scritti*, pp. 752–754.

follows the relevant principle taught by Fr. Vallée during the retreat he preached in 1900. The Dominican called to mind the behavior of the saints before God: "They are silent, recollected, and do not involve themselves with any activity besides that of souls [Elizabeth writes 'beings'] who receive."[166]

This principle became a formative theme in the strengthening of Elizabeth's desire to remain near the wellspring in order to receive and therefore be able to give, and it reappears in her writings as a recurrent melody dear to her heart.

Echoes of her Thérèsian readings mingle with her own reflections and other ideas read or remembered from Fr. Vallée's preaching; for example, her reference to the attitude of *listening*, even to the point of speaking of a passion for listening to what God says to the soul.[167]

This is made clear in her question to André Chevignard: "Don't you have a passion for listening to" the Maestro, Christ? It is this the duty of the priest, "the contemplative" who "lives under the brilliance of the face of Christ, who enters into the mystery of God, not into the light that comes from human thought, but into the light of the word that emanates from the incarnate Word."

It is from listening to that which emanates from the Word that the need to keep silent is born. "One would want to know how to do nothing else beside remain, like the Magdalen, ... at the feet of the Maestro, desirous of understanding to the depths, penetrating always more intimately this mystery of charity that [Christ] has come to reveal to us."

[166] To André Chevignard, L165, June 14, 1903. The original says: "Ils ... n'ont d'activite que pour être l'être qui recoit."

[167] During the retreat of 1900, Fr. Vallée had said: the soul "vient avec la passion d'entendre; elle est la tout entire pour ecouter." Cf. *J'ai trouvé Dieu*, vol. Ib, 3, p. 150.

And her thoughts go to St. Teresa of Ávila's *Interior Castle*, in which the roles of Martha and Mary are seen together: "Doesn't it seem to you that during activity, when one takes the part of Martha, the soul can always rest adoring, buried like the Magdalen in her contemplation, attached to this wellspring like one who is thirsty?"[168]

The key to reading this passage can be found in conformity to Christ, in the participation of the human person with His life in us, by which the progressive divinization of all the soul's movements advances in the soul. Christ is present; He transforms every human activity from inside, and it does not matter whether it is a moment of contemplation or an hour of physical activity (which, of course, cannot fully absorb the faculties of the intellect and will of the person).

The apostolic fruitfulness of contemplative prayer depends on this total identification with Christ. It does not depend on a psychological effort to unite contemplation and activity, as is sometimes thought when spending time with people dedicated to cloistered contemplative life. From the moment she understands the meaning of her own name, "house of God," Elizabeth understands that everything connects with the presence of the "divine Adorer" in her, that everything is tied to the strict union of her life with the divine life in her. Therefore when she prays, it is He who prays within her; it is He who "thirsts greatly to identify us with all that He is and to transform us into Himself."[169]

---

[168] To André Chevignard, L158, February 24, 1903, in *Gli Scritti*, pp. 241–242.

[169] To Germana de Gemeaux, L179, September 20, 1903, in *Gli Scritti*, p. 273.

The poetic expression of Elizabeth's thought abounds with thematic reflections that are even more evocative than the expressions she uses in her letters.

At Christmas, desiring to spend her "life listening to the Word" present in her, "house of God," she can say:

> Within I have the prayer
> of Jesus Christ, divine Adorer.
> This carries me toward souls and the Father,
> for this is His double movement.
> My *mission* is that
> of *being, with my Maestro, Savior.*
> For this I must disappear
> and lose myself in Him
> because I am united to Him.
> Jesus, Word of life,
> united to You forever,
> may Your virgin and host
> shine out love:
> Amo Christum![170]

Union with Christ, love of Christ, saving souls with Him: anything is possible for one who is a "house of God," in which Christ carries the prayers up to the Father and at the same time moves toward souls.

And so there seems to have been born a new creature, both contemplative and apostolic.

---

[170] Poem 88, December 25, 1903, in *Gli Scritti*, p. 755 (author's translation and emphasis).

For Elizabeth it is easy to find a reference in Mary. "Mother of the Word, tell me your mystery," she asks in the same poem, so that the Virgin Mary might teach her, like Mary and with her, to "carry within, the imprint of this God–All Love" to give Him to souls.

This drawing near to Mary sheds a new light on Elizabeth's desire to be a bride of Christ and a mother of souls, "mediator with Christ," and as such, to be for Him "an extra-added humanity, in which He can perpetuate His life of reparation . . . of praise and adoration."[171] It is therefore correct to say that the Dijon Carmelite had a sacramental understanding of her own life.[172]

In fact, the 1904 Christmas poem ends with the sincere and joyful assertion: "My heart becomes Your lowly sacrament."[173]

A few months earlier she had written in her *Personal Notes*: "The Carmelite is a sacrament of Christ."[174]

But this means that the Carmelite is an ecclesial creature, a living member of the Church, who is Christ's sacrament, an apostolic creature mysteriously identified with the sacramental Church, a contemplative who continuously draws from the divine wellspring, making herself a sacrament of Christ's grace and mercy.

---

[171] To Canon Angles, L256, end of December 1905, in *J'ai trouvé Dieu*, vol. Ib, p. 327.

[172] Sicari, *Elisabetta*, p. 146.

[173] Poem 91, December 25, 1904, in *Gli Scritti*, p. 737. In French: "Mon coeur deviant votre humble sacrement."

[174] *Personal Notes*, 14, second half of 1903, in *J'ai trouvé Dieu*, vol. II, p. 124.

CHAPTER FOUR

A SPIRITUALITY
FOR TODAY

Elizabeth of the Trinity's relevance consists in her Christian, spiritual, gospel message.

There is nothing extraordinary in her life.

There were no ecstasies; she didn't work miracles; she didn't
communicate words heard, revelations, or heavenly messages, like
those found in her contemporary Gemma Galgani (1878–1903).

Elizabeth presented a message and teaching that were simply
her own life of fidelity to her vocation, profoundly rooted in her
baptismal graces, lived in the light of the word of God and the
ascetic-mystical doctrine of Carmel.

Before all else there was the word of God. Elizabeth cited it
often, not to explain it, but to pour it out into the hearts of the
recipients of her letters. It didn't even cross her mind to attempt
a theological explanation. She was certain that the Holy Spirit
would intervene to bring to life the divine word: it was enough
to listen to it, as she did, allowing oneself to be wrapped in it,
educated by it, to be raised up by it. But this word served also
to speak about her self, her spiritual journey, and her great and
passionate love for Christ.

With the biblical word she "revealed" the intimate secrets of her heart, knowing that no other explanation was necessary: she felt "explained" by the word, and she was happy.

Reading the Gospels and the Pauline writings, Elizabeth came into contact with the mysteries of the Faith. Some of these illuminated her journey in a particular way: the indwelling of the Three Divine Persons in the soul; Jesus Christ, incarnate Word, the way to the Father, to the praise and glory of the Trinity.

Her "discovery" of St. Paul's letters in the Scriptures assumed great importance. At the Dijon monastery, on a few cards, are preserved indications of the ideas and themes that interested her from Paul's writings. These show that in her free time she dedicated herself to a study of the doctrine of her "dear St. Paul," as she used to call him.

It seems that some of these texts were so strongly impressed on her mind that she could write them from memory. She meditated on them for long periods, assimilating the contents like secret melodies; often repeated as love songs with Eternal Love. Then she transmitted the truths understood, not so as to fill the pages of her letters, but making them the very "substance" of her letters.

It is in this light that her final *Retreats*, laboriously prepared in her humble cell in the infirmary, ought to be read and understood. In the prayerful silence of that cell, the truths of the Pauline teaching about "the mystery hidden for ages" set her aflame with love and gave her the strength to bear atrocious pains, almost forgetting them, and raised her astonished gaze toward the Infinite, toward the beloved Being who is above every other creature.

It is moving to think that only a few days before her death, in a thank-you letter (dictated due to her extreme weakness) she wanted to explain to her doctor, Dr. Barbier, the significance the Pauline letters held for her:

> In this final hour of my exile, in this beautiful evening of my life, how everything appears to me in light of eternity!... I would like to shout to all souls and tell them the vanity, the nothingness of all that happens without having been done for God. At least I am certain to be heard by your soul, dear good doctor who has always understood me so well. I was always aware of that, and I was happy in the depth of my heart. Oh! Return often to those things we discussed together [she refers to their frequent spiritual conversations about the Pauline teachings] and allow your soul to resonate under the breath of that grace that they breathe over you.

Doesn't this echo the biblical word: "Like a spring rain it does not return without having watered the earth"? (cf. Isa. 55:10–11).

> It gave me great joy to see that you appreciated my dear St. Paul, and I ask you to accept, in order to complete my joy, a final goodbye from your little patient, and as a final testimony of her affectionate gratitude, a book of these Letters, from which my soul received great strength in trial. We will meet again in the light that these pages shine on those who read them with the faith of the children of God. In this light, which for me will soon have no shadows, I will remember you.[175]

This letter illustrates clearly the profound rootedness in the Scriptures of Elizabeth's spiritual doctrine.

[175] To Dr. Barbier, L340, early November 1906, in *Gli Scritti*, p. 500.

"You need to listen to her, without interrupting her, without tak-ing offense at her repetition." Dr. Barbier and the others who came to the monastery to speak with the young monastic did just that.

> She ventures into the word of St. Paul with the non-chalance of the children of God; she allows herself to be wounded in the deepest part of her heart by the blows of this word, with a blessed serenity that has no part in anxiety nor the terrors that plagued the spirited, from Augustine to Gottschalk through the Reformers and the Jansenists; before all these she sinks into the abyss of the mystery.[176]

This is the judgment of Hans Urs von Balthasar.

Elizabeth teaches how Scripture is to be read and meditated upon, not by being occupied simply with the scientific [theologi-cal] considerations. And with a child's simplicity she abandons herself into the arms of her Father, in the joy of one who loves God and wants to adore Him.

In her constant effort to listen to the word of God, Elizabeth teaches how to pray *with* the word of God.

Her great need to love, in a certain way "to feel and grasp" God, whom she feels near, is the door to sharing her feelings using this divine word, exalting it in a climate of silence and solitude. That which her "dear St. Paul"—an expression found in her writ-ings—"tells" her, often becomes a filial prayer, an invocation, a declaration of love, a thanksgiving, and above all, praise.

Praise is a typical and unmistakable aspect of biblical prayer.

Intuited with the help of a particular grace formulated in the Pauline hymn in Ephesians 1:3–14, Elizabeth's prayer of praise

---

[176] Hans Urs von Balthasar, *Suor Elisabetta della Trinità* (Milano, 1959), p. 34.

has as its object the whole arc of the Christian mystery: predestination, adoration, God's infinite greatness, recognition of His glorious manifestations — which light in her soul the ecstasy of admiration together with the unending flow of gratitude.

Her new name, *Laudem Gloriae*, expresses the amen of her faith and of her love, sung on the lyre of contemplation of the marvelous works of God.

Elizabeth carries her readers toward bold abandonment and immersion in God, connecting them to the eternal praise of the saints in heaven.

It is Christian prayer's privilege to "render thanks joyously to the Father who qualified us to share in the inheritance of the saints in light" (cf. Col. 1:12), a privilege of freedom from constraints and from mediocrity in order to be drawn out of oneself into divine contemplation. In any case, it is not a prayer that rests exclusively in the heights of the mystery of God.

Rather, the glory of God shines in the Church and in Jesus Christ, made a man like us. Elizabeth keeps this in mind, even though she doesn't fully bring it to light.

Not only the prayer of praise, but every prayer with the word of God focuses on the Word Incarnate and hopes to enter into the sanctuary of Jesus' personal life — there where, in sublime and unrepeatable moments, heaven and earth, God and humanity, meet.

In the questionnaire completed by Elizabeth Catez at her entrance at Carmel there appears this question: "Which is your favorite book?" Her answer is very simple: "The soul of Christ; this confides all the secrets of the Father who art in heaven."

In the soul of Christ Elizabeth encounters and reads the mystery of God through intimate participation in His prayer of adoration and reparation. In Jesus she sees the gift of our adoptive sonship realized, a gift that establishes in us the culmination of the salvific work wrought in the person of the Incarnate Son.

In Him she knows she has been brought into the filial relationship that unites the Christian to the Divine Persons and transforms him into a new creation.

Incorporated into Christ, even "in the dark nights of the spirit," Elizabeth, as a new creation, draws near to the Father, to God the Trinity, with filial affection because she is convinced that Christ prays in her, making her a participant of His own prayer, of the conversation between the resurrected Jesus and the Father.

This gives rise to her desire to feel "invaded" by Christ: that He is present in her like an interior and effective power, substituting Himself for her soul so that she might disappear in Him, to create a mysterious unity between Christ's life and hers.

This personal and formative indwelling of Christ in her, akin to "another Incarnation of the Word" in her soul, which is a divine gift worked by the presence of the Holy Spirit, opens the doors to the divine sanctuary of the Trinitarian relationships.

Assimilated into Christ, penetrated by the fire of the Holy Spirit, the Dijon Carmelite, with the invocation "Father, bend down over this little creature," casts herself upon her Three, "Blessedness and infinite Solitude."[177]

The importance of this doctrine for our own spiritual lives must not be underestimated.

It is the living expression, a reflection of the Trinitarian dimension of the Faith that we often neglect, of a truth rooted in baptism: we Christians, regenerated by the Holy Spirit and

---

[177] "Hymn to the Trinity," November 2, 1904, in *Gli Scritti*, pp. 605–606.

clothed with Christ, are admitted to Trinitarian intimacy. In other words, in hearing the word of God and in prayer with the word of God, we are called to bring to effect, sometimes even unintentionally, the baptismal grace that makes us Christians. Putting this grace into effect brings us, by virtue of our union with Christ and in the docility of the inspiration of the Holy Spirit, to live in the presence of the Trinitarian God.

Elizabeth Catez, with her life and experience, reminds us of the right and the capacity we have as a "new humanity" and "adopted sons" to draw near with faith, audacity, and love to the great Christian truth of the Trinitarian indwelling. It is not necessary to examine it by theological study. For Elizabeth, a brief explanation by Fr. Vallée on the revealed truth using God's own word was enough.

We know that she remained indifferent to the exegetical gifts of interpretation of the Dominican father, drifting off immediately to other places, preferring to live the mystery and abandoning herself to her Three in a secret conversation of adoration and love.

It is her profound love that begets the prayer "O my God, Trinity whom I adore": an inexplicable masterpiece of abstract reflection, yet spoken with the creative power of the word of God, assimilated and raised to heaven with expressions born of a profound ecstasy of loving words experienced in the intimate depths [of her soul].

All of this shows that in Elizabeth Catez we have a guide for the Trinitarian orientation of our lives and for Christian prayer. We are a temple, dwelling, living icon of the Triune God thanks to our baptismal vocation, to our Christian personality.

The Carmelite of Dijon made use of the doctrine of the great saints of her order to effect her immersion in the Trinitarian mystery with greater understanding and increasing perfection. Her contemplative apostolate flows from Carmelite doctrine, and it is in light of this doctrine that we can develop her teachings. We need to affirm that the letters of Teresa of Ávila, Thérèse of Lisieux, and John of the Cross were for Elizabeth preparation, support, encouragement, and confirmation of her own spirit.

To highlight the importance of the great ascetical themes of silence, solitude, and imitation of Christ crucified, as well as the meaning of growth in the love of God, she drew inspiration from works such as *The Way of Perfection* and *The Story of a Soul*. She insists on hiding herself in the mystery of God; and with the "Father of Carmel" she advances on the way of naked faith without sensible consolations. "St. John of the Cross tells us that [the faith] serves as the basis for going to God and that it represents the possession in a state of darkness [literally: of truth in a darkened state], that this alone can shine true light on Him whom we love, and that we have to welcome it as the way to arrive at blessed union."[178]

This teaching about the life of faith is fundamental for our times. Modern man and woman are no less exposed than their medieval counterparts to the temptations of false mysticism, of the dramatic intervention of the divine in daily life.

Elizabeth, on the other hand, had no other God than the God revealed in and through Jesus Christ, the one and triune God of the Bible, who lowers Himself toward mankind, going beyond what man could even hope for. But the God of faith demands total faithfulness beyond all understanding.

---

[178] *Heaven in Faith*, 6.1, August 1906, in *Gli Scritti*, p. 618.

Up until the final moments of her life, Elizabeth bore the darkness of faith with exemplary patience—a faith that excluded every other love, preference, or satisfaction in order to orient her solely toward God-Love, in a serene expectancy of His coming. "The faith is so beautiful. It is heaven in shadows."[179] And her faith became praise, sacrifice, and the choice of a humble and poor life.

During the trials of her illness, it was faith that infused the strength to accept her pain and exhaustion, the sense of abandonment by God, the experience of emptiness, and the relentless torment of hunger and thirst. She might have thrown herself from the window without the support of faith. The temptation to suicide was truly present in her at an hour of exceptional desolation, and we know that Thérèse of Lisieux knew similar trials, which are part of the martyrdom of faith.

Elizabeth raised her gaze to the crucified Bridegroom.

If she had asked to participate in the sufferings of Christ, to be transformed into His image, was this not the moment in which He answered her?

"The Lord does not forget any of those things that can help make me like Him. It is His action that I am undergoing"[180]—an action she received courageously. In her there existed no other way than to be "conformed to the divine Maestro on the Cross." And under the powerful hand of God, she continued to suffer "the interminable nights of purification while awaiting her death." To those who saw her thusly abandoned and "vigilant in faith," the passive force with which she bore her slow martyrdom almost

---

[179] To her Rolland aunts, L162, April 28–30, 1903, in *Gli Scritti*, p. 244.

[180] *Summarium*, p. 70, no. 152.

seemed more impressive "than her strength in bearing the dreadful sufferings" in the moments of crisis.[181]

Already on the night of the vigil of her Profession, finding herself "in the choir waiting for the Bridegroom, I understood that my heaven began on earth, the heaven of faith, with the suffering and immolation for Him whom I love."[182] So she wrote to Canon Angles in 1903 after the time of her first purification and night of darkness, a time of interior sufferings, but not yet physical.

Having arrived at the final chapter of her life, the heaven of faith "makes her rise to that God 'who works every thing with the counsel of His will' ... and this will, at times crucifying, never ceases to be entirely love."[183]

But even this second heaven is, in Elizabeth, a heaven of love.

God always reveals Himself as love, and this is true even at the hour in which the Father places His Son on the Cross. We must believe this; Elizabeth knew how to do so.

"The heroism of this trial, so blessed by God, is a powerful call to faith, naked and pure, the foundation of the Christian life," said the postulator of her cause for beatification. She would never have desired to distance herself from humble fidelity to a life founded upon faith. She desired "to welcome, moment by moment, that which God desires and prepares." Citing the deposition of one of the most qualified and intimate of the witnesses, he adds that Elizabeth "was the life of faith in all its simplicity."[184]

---

[181] Ibid., p. 81, no. 180.

[182] To Canon Angles, L169, July 15, 1903, in *Gli Scritti*, p. 255.

[183] To the Baroness d'Anthès, L257, early January 1906, in *Gli Scritti*, p. 398.

[184] Macca, *Elisabetta*, p. 51; cf. *Summarium*, p. 396, no. 826.

This simplicity was manifest not only in her life of faith.

Diligence in making herself simple, humble, and obedient accompanied her efforts to be an authentic Carmelite, a true daughter and reflection of God. "I want that in seeing me, God is thought of." This was not a random afterthought in a conversation; it was what actually happened.[185]

Anyone who met her felt himself to be in the presence of a woman who loved God passionately in the "simplicity that brings Him honor and praise, that presents and offers Him the virtues."[186] That is, she continued to fulfill carefully, "with every possible perfection," as Teresa of Ávila told her, animated by faith, hope, and charity, that which God asks of every Christian every day, including the most ordinary acts.

Drawing inspiration from Ruusbroec, she found in simplicity that attitude "which will increase our divine resemblance by the hour ... and will lead us into the depths where God lives.... The simple soul, 'elevating itself by virtue of its interior glance, enters into itself and contemplates in its own abyss the sanctuary where it has blossomed' by the touch of the Holy Trinity. In this way the soul is understood in its depths, to its very bottom, which is the door to eternal life."[187]

More than a destination at which to arrive, these words, copied from Hello's anthology, are the confirmation of a lifelong heroic effort to be truly simple. Considering Elizabeth's character, one can appreciate the difficulty she encountered.

---

[185] *Summarium*, p. 106, no. 242.

[186] *Heaven in Faith*, 6.2, August 1906, in *Gli Scritti*, p. 619. The original Italian text seems to have a typographical error, dating the text "August 1903." — Trans.

[187] Ibid., pp. 619–620.

The testimonies left by her fellow Carmelite sisters agree that there was a continual growth in virtue in Elizabeth, a constant ascent to arrive at perfect self-mastery, to be able to give to others without drawing attention to herself or to her acts of charity, which were done simply and promptly with love.

Elizabeth had to gather up all her interior strength to hold her attention on God in the midst of her daily routine and to avoid speaking of the difficulties she encountered. She didn't lose herself in useless things, but abandoned herself to the interior action of the Holy Spirit with an increasingly sure and clear awareness of God-Trinity in her life. To this presence, experienced in gospel simplicity, were anchored her contemplative existence in the Church and her spiritual teachings.

It is right to want to call hers a "living spirituality," derived as it is from an ecclesial experience and from wisdom of the word of God, carried out with the help of her baptismal grace and free from any search for the extraordinary.

A spirituality like hers is relevant, constructive, and therefore valid for today's Christian, both because it is expressed in light of biblical, liturgical, and theological elements, and because it is identical to a life lived in faith and love, in absolute simplicity, by God's true children.

SELECTED BIBLIOGRAPHY

SOURCES

Elisabetta parla ancora. Care of General Postulator. Roma, 1980.

Elisabetta della Trinità racconta la sua vita. Care of Conrad de Meester. Roma, 1984.

Elisabetta della Trinità. *Opere I* (care of Luigi Borriello). Cinisello Balsamo, 1993.

Elizabeth of the Trinity. *[Gli] Scritti*, OCD, Roma, 1967.

―――. *J'ai trouvé Dieu. Oeuvres complètes*. (Edition realize, présenté, annotée par Conrad de Meester, Carme). Vol. II: Diary, Personal Notes, Letters from Her Youth, Poems. Paris, 1979.

―――. *J'ai trouvé Dieu. Oeuvres complètes*. (Edition realize, présenté, annotée par Conrad de Meester, Carme). Vol Ia: General Introduction, Spiritual Traits; and vol. Ib: Letters from Carmel. Paris, 1980.

Germaine de Jésus. *Souvenir de soeur Elisabeth de la Trinité*. Dijon, 1915. (Italian trans. *Elisabetta della Trinità. Ricordi*. 8th ed. Roma, 1984.

STUDIES

Ardens. *Un balzo nel divino.* Roma, 1983.

Balthasar, Hans Urs von. *Sorelle nello Spirito, Teresa di Lisieux e Elisabetta della Trinità.* Milano, 1974.

Borriello, Luigi. *Elisabetta della Trinità, Una vocazione realizzata secondo il progetto di Dio.* Napoli, 1980.

DeMeester, Conrad. *Elisabeth von Dijon. Ich gehe zum Licht. Leben und Erfahrungen im Selbstzeugnis.* Freiburg, 1984.

Elisabetta della Trinità—Esperienza e dottrina. Roma, 1980.

Ho creduto al Dio presente. Torino, 1971.

Lafrance, Jean. *Imoarare a pregare con Suor Elisabetta della Trinità,* Milano, 1985. Trans. from the French, Paris, 1964.

L'esperienza mistica di Elisabetta della Trinità. Napoli, 1987.

Llamas, Enrique. *Dios en nosotros: doctrina spiritual de Sor Isabel de la Trinidad.* Madrid, 1969.

Macca, Valentino. *Elisabetta della Trinità. Un esperienza di grazia nel cuore della Chiesa.* Roma, 1976.

Moretti, Roberto. *Introduzione a Elisabetta della Trinità. Vita—Scritti—Dottrina.* Roma 1984.

Philipon, M.M. *L'inabitazione della Trinità nell'anima. La spiritualità di Elisabetta della Trinità.* Milano, 1966.

———. *La dottrina spirituale di sour Elisabetta della Trinità,* 9th ed. Brescia, 1983.

Poinsenet, Marie-Dominique. *Questa presenza di Dio in te.* Milano, 1971.

Sicari, Antonio. *Elisabetta della Trinità. Un'esistenza teologica.* Roma, 1984.

SPIRITUAL DIRECTION
⫸ SERIES ⫷

SOPHIA INSTITUTE PRESS

If this book has caused a stir in your heart to continue to pursue your relationship with God, we invite you to explore two extraordinary resources, SpiritualDirection.com and the Avila Institute for Spiritual Formation.

The readers of SpiritualDirection.com reside in almost every country of the world where hearts yearn for God. It is the world's most popular English site dedicated to authentic Catholic spirituality.

The Students of the Avila Institute for Spiritual Formation sit at the feet of the rich and deep well of the wisdom of the saints.

You can find more about the Avila Institute at
WWW.AVILA-INSTITUTE.COM.

Sophia Institute

Sophia Institute is a nonprofit institution that seeks to nurture the spiritual, moral, and cultural life of souls and to spread the Gospel of Christ in conformity with the authentic teachings of the Roman Catholic Church.

Sophia Institute Press fulfills this mission by offering translations, reprints, and new publications that afford readers a rich source of the enduring wisdom of mankind.

Sophia Institute also operates two popular online Catholic resources: CrisisMagazine.com and CatholicExchange.com.

Crisis Magazine provides insightful cultural analysis that arms readers with the arguments necessary for navigating the ideological and theological minefields of the day. *Catholic Exchange* provides world news from a Catholic perspective as well as daily devotionals and articles that will help you to grow in holiness and live a life consistent with the teachings of the Church.

In 2013, Sophia Institute launched Sophia Institute for Teachers to renew and rebuild Catholic culture through service to Catholic education. With the goal of nurturing the spiritual, moral, and cultural life of souls, and an abiding respect for the role and work of teachers, we strive to provide materials and programs that are at once enlightening to the mind and ennobling to the heart; faithful and complete, as well as useful and practical.

Sophia Institute gratefully recognizes the Solidarity Association for preserving and encouraging the growth of our apostolate over the course of many years. Without their generous and timely support, this book would not be in your hands.

www.SophiaInstitute.com
www.CatholicExchange.com
www.CrisisMagazine.com
www.SophiaInstituteforTeachers.org

Sophia Institute Press® is a registered trademark of Sophia Institute.
Sophia Institute is a tax-exempt institution as defined by the
Internal Revenue Code, Section 501(c)(3). Tax I.D. 22-2548708.